Light Beyond the Darkness

The compelling story of how one child through God's grace found the strength to forgive her parents after many years of emotional abuse.

T.C. Morton

Published by
Solid Rock Publishing
P.O. Box 913
Stillwater, MN 55082

Jean—
Praise God for He
turns all things to
His Glory!
Col 3:16-17
T. Chris Morton

Solid Rock Publishing
P.O. Box 913
Stillwater, MN 55082

ISBN 0-9657118-0-3
LCCN 96-093139

Printed by Ideal Printers, Inc. St. Paul MN

This Book contains the memories of T.C. Morton. The
intention of writing this book was not meant to hurt or
harm any person mentioned by her. There was no malicious
intentions and therefore she can not be held legally bound
by any such statements that she remembers. Some names
have been substituted are changed.

"But you are a chosen people... belonging to God, that you may declare the praises of him who called you out of darkness and into his wonderful light."
1 Peter 2:9

Light Beyond the Darkness

Contents

Preface

Chapter 1.   My First Memory

Chapter 2.   The Next Day

Chapter 3.   The Good Side of Mama

Chapter 4.   A Real Surprise

Chapter 5.   The Car Accident

Chapter 6.   Mama's Boyfriend

Chapter 7.   The Motel

Chapter 8.   Without A Goodbye

Chapter 9.   Homestead, Florida

Chapter 10.   Preschool

Chapter 11.   Bradenton, Florida

Chapter 12.   The Boy's Rug

Chapter 13.   Sanford, Florida

Chapter 14.   The Good Life

Chapter 15.   A Part of Mama I Loved

Chapter 16.   Broken Promises

Chapter 17.   Stitches, This Time in the Head

Chapter 18.   Learning to Ride

Chapter 19.   Guest for Dinner

Chapter 20.   Stabbed with the Screwdriver

Chapter 21.   Accident on the Bridge

Chapter 22.   Dangerous Fresh Water

Chapter 23.   Stupie

Chapter 24.   The Day I Made Friends with Jesus

Chapter 25.   What A Horrible Birthday

Chapter 26.   Choo-Choo

Chapter 27.   Sounds Like A Fresh Start

Chapter 28.   Our New House in Palma Sola Florida

Chapter 29.   Misleading Games

Chapter 30.   Nod My Head and Smile

Chapter 31.   Don't Speak Louder Than A Whisper

Chapter 32.   "Baby"

Chapter 33.   Christmas Eve

Chapter 34.   Where's Daddy?

Chapter 35.   Something We Did Everyday

Chapter 36.   A Real Lesson in Piano

Chapter 37.   Walking in Darkness

Chapter 38.   Grandma's Surprise

Chapter 39.   Daddy's Tears

Chapter 40.   Please Don't Die Mama

Chapter 41.   Broken Arm

Chapter 42.   Mama's Boyfriend Horace

Chapter 43.   Adventures On Our Boat

Chapter 44.   To Catch A Shark

Chapter 45.   Truth or Dare

Chapter 46.   Mama's New Car

Chapter 47.   Why Did I Do That?

Chapter 48.   "Help Me! She Shot Me!"

Chapter 49.   I Wanted To Forget It All

Chapter 50. Never Tell Family Secrets

Chapter 51. Through The Darkness, God Was
There

Chapter 52. Just To Be Cool

Chapter 53. Bad Choices

Chapter 54. I Walked On Eggshells Day After Day

Chapter 55. The Eggshells Cracked

Chapter 56. Christmas Without Daddy

Chapter 57. Mama Remarried

Chapter 58. There Was No Sign Of Life

Chapter 59. Mama's Fourth Husband

Chapter 60. Summer In Crown Point, Indiana

Chapter 61. Returning Home

Chapter 62. Moving Again

Chapter 63. St. Petersburg, Florida

Chapter 64. The White Witch

Chapter 65. The Perfect Family

Chapter 66. Feeling Empty

Chapter 67. Panic

Chapter 68. Living With Butch

Chapter 69. Torn Between the Joy of Christmas and
The Feeling of Being Abandoned

Chapter 70. Moved to Texas

Chapter 71. Black Magic

Chapter 72 The Truth

Chapter 73 God Works All Things for The Good

Epilogue

Light Beyond the Darkness

Dedication

This book, in deep appreciation, is dedicated to:

-My Savior Jesus Christ, who set the example of forgiveness.

Light Beyond the Darkness

Acknowledgments

Foremost, I want my mom to know that I love her very much and forgive any wrong doing and appreciate all the good qualities that she has passed on through parenting. Even though we endured many hard times, I love her and honor her. The Bible tells us to Honor our Mother and Father. There is no disclaimer in the Bible about how they should act in order to obtain our respect; it's a given respect regardless of actions or deeds. The key to obeying this important commandment in some cases is forgiveness. There was pain in my past but more importantly there was were many fond memories and so many important lessons she that she taught me about life- and the most important single gift my mom gave me was that of the knowledge of salvation through Jesus Christ.

Mama also taught me the importance of forgiveness. She herself has shown forgiveness to family members that hurt her as a child and she not only shows forgiveness but when "her enemies" ask for her coat she gives them her shirt too.

There are so many other people to thank! Thanks to all who took the time to preview this book and encourage me to continue on: Kim Smith, Lois Lindeman, Nancy Moore, Mike & Molly Smith, Pastor Leonard J. Nadeau, Angela Kline, Leanne Sorteberg, and Lisa Ragsdale, Deb Jacobe, Lynn & Larry Lindahl and to Colleen Morchinek for helping me come up with the title. A super special thanks goes to Lori Hoganson and Julie and Mark Johnson for listening to the Lord and offering their help toward the publication of this book!

For encouraging every step of the way I thank my husband Tom and oldest daughter Meredith. Thank you for enduring me when the writing got tough! And for helping me grow into a better person, wife and mother.

Thank you to all those who have prayed for this book to become a reality. My prayer is that it will bless someone, as well as, make a difference in their relationship with others and more importantly with Jesus Christ.

Preface

When I was a little girl, each night I said my prayers before going to bed. There were many nights that I asked God to just let me die in my sleep. I didn't want to awaken to yet another agonizing day. I thought it would be easier to just give up and die than to deal with the pain and suffering that I went through each and every day.

Both my parents were alcoholics. Our home was filled with abusive language, fighting, and emotional anguish. Now I know that God didn't plan for me, or anyone else, to experience the pain associated with abuse, but what He <u>did</u> plan was a way for us to endure the suffering, to forgive and walk in the path of righteousness. He gave me the strength to endure the pain and eventually find a way out of it (1 Corinthians 10:13).

As you read through the journal of my life from age three to thirteen, you may see yourself. You may be reminded of your own past. This book is going to walk you through the darkness of abuse that I experienced. What I hope you walk away <u>with</u> is the hope, the forgiveness, and most importantly, the faithfulness of God to guide us <u>all</u> out of the darkness.

Light Beyond the Darkness

1
Summer, 1968   My First Memory

It all began in the summer of 1968. We lived in a small, white brick house on the east side of town. It wasn't a rich neighborhood but, as a child, I didn't know the difference. Neighbors existed on each side of our house. Across the street there were acres of woods. It was scary to think about what might come out of those woods at night.

Bradenton, Florida, is often hot and humid at night. Sometimes we could feel the breeze, but mid-summer most often meant warm and sticky night air. We always wanted an air conditioner; instead, we made do with fans and open windows. In our living room was a vinyl couch. When we stood up, we could feel the sweat as it gathered behind our knees and ran down the back of our legs.

One particular night, my brothers and I were home alone. Butch, age 12, and George, age 10, and I, age 3, had a choice of going to the bar with our parents or staying home alone. That was a typical option for us. Given the choice, we would much rather stay at home.

Our parents went out for a drink or two and were only going to be out for a little while. Even at the age of three, I already understood what my parents meant when they said a "drink or two." I knew that it would be late before they were home. It was always a challenge for me to stay up until they got home. I fought the sandman and tried desperately to stay awake.

Our little white house had five rooms: two small bedrooms, a bathroom, kitchen and living room. Mama and Daddy and I shared the largest of the two bedrooms. On one side of the room was my parents' bed. On the opposite wall, next to the open window, was my bed. I hated sleeping next to the window. I was scared of the woods and scared of someone breaking into our house. My brothers shared the other bedroom that was across the narrow, tile-floored hall. We had moved around quite a bit and, though this house was small, I liked it because during the day I loved playing in our fenced in back yard.

It was pitch black outside, and we had opened up all the windows to let some breeze into the house. My brothers tried to get me to go to bed, but I was scared to sleep alone in the bedroom. So, in total darkness, the boys and I sat on the couch and watched television. Butch was on one end of the couch and George on the other, and I stretched out between the two. Butch was rubbing my feet and George was resting his arm on my shoulder. I felt comfortable and with the people who loved me the most. The boys were quiet and the television's volume was low. We were prepared for the moment that Mama and Daddy came home. We had been home alone many times before, so we knew what to do when they arrived. The plan was to run to our rooms, jump into bed, and pretend to be asleep.

As I lay on the couch trying to stay awake, I knew the minute that I fell asleep one of my brothers would carry me into the bedroom and leave me there all alone. As my eyes drifted shut, my body suddenly jolted up as I heard my parents' car pull up under the carport. I could feel my heart begin to race, and, before I could jump up to go, George was on his feet and dragging me up with him. "I hope they aren't fighting," he whispered as he rushed me off to my room. Without turning on the light, he quickly tucked me into bed and surrounded me from head to toe with stuffed animals. I was so scared to sleep next to the window that I kept my bed full of stuffed animals. Each night before I went to sleep, I would put the animals all around me and on top of me to protect me as I slept. It looked like a pile of toys instead of a little girl sleeping. As we heard the car doors slam, George kissed me quickly on the forehead and said "No matter what, pretend like you're asleep!"

As I lay there with my eyes open in the dark room, I heard Mama and Daddy standing on the front lawn arguing. I tried not to move. If Mama saw me awake, the boys and I would get in trouble, yet I was too frightened to stay in the room alone. I listened to my parents on the lawn arguing. Why didn't they come in the house? What was going on out there? Through the open window I listened to them fight.

My heart began to pound. It was terrible when my parents fought. They screamed, hit, and nearly killed each other. Finally, I couldn't take it any longer, and regardless of my brother's warning, I discarded the animals, climbed out of bed, and tiptoed down the hall. Despite the heat of the night air, the floor was cold to my bare feet. I peeked around the corner into the living room.

The television was off and the boys were sitting on the couch, on their knees. They were facing the window that looked out onto the front yard. With their backs to me, they were peeking through the curtains. The boys were so intensely spying on Mama and Daddy that they didn't hear me come into the room. When Butch noticed that Mama was turning towards the house, he let go of the curtain. As he flipped around to get up, he saw me standing there. He was completely at a loss for words. His eyes became wide and his mouth dropped open, for he knew that Mama would beat us both if she found me awake. He grabbed me by the arm and pulled me over to the couch. I thought he was going to rush me back to my room. It was too late to run down the hall. Instead, he quickly searched the room for a hiding spot. I guess he was trying to save me from a beating. Gritting his teeth, he said, "Get under the couch, NOW!" I did so immediately. Our couch sat up on pedestal legs, and I had just enough room to squeeze underneath it. Butch lay down on the couch and pretended to be asleep.

Under the couch the tile was cool, damp and dusty. How could I be cold? It was eighty-five degrees in the house. It was a tight squeeze underneath there, and the cloth that covered the bottom of the couch sagged onto my head. It tickled my cheek and reminded me of the tiny, brown roaches that also lived in our house. If you walked into the kitchen at night and turned on the light, you could see hundreds of them just scatter across the counters. Thinking about the roaches as I lay there in the dark on the floor, I decided the wrath of Mama was better then a hundred roaches crawling all over my body. I crawled out from underneath the couch. Fortunately, Mama didn't come in that time.

Butch and I ran back to his room and there the three of us sat on the bed. We were all so afraid because the fighting continued and was getting worse. We sat quietly. Daddy came storming into the house. He rushed into his bedroom and thank goodness, he didn't notice me missing. We heard him throwing drawers open and throwing things around. George gave me a stern look. I knew what he was thinking. He was thinking that we were all going to get in trouble, because I was supposed to be in my bed. Daddy didn't notice. He probably thought that I was somewhere amongst my stuffed animals. Mama came in and was in the living room. I heard two loud "clicks," then dad stomped down the hall. In the living room Daddy dropped something on the tiled floor that sounded like glass crashing. Mama began cursing Daddy. Suddenly, I heard the loudest noise I had ever heard in my life. It was the blast of Daddy's double-barrel shotgun.

Everything seemed to stop. For a second, the world was peacefully quiet. Then the boys jumped up and ran down the hall to see if Mama was okay. I followed in their footsteps to the living room. Butch and

George were crouched behind the kitchen bar counter, and Mama and Daddy were wrestling over the gun. In the middle of the room was what used to be a plastic clothes basket containing Mama's clothes and stuff. It was now blown to pieces all over the floor. George motioned me to his side. Mama was yelling at Daddy about how she was going to kill him for destroying her stuff and ruining her life. With the gun in hand Daddy walked out of the front door.

The boys decided enough was enough; it was time to run away. I didn't want to run away, but I didn't want to stay there and watch my parents kill each other either, so I left with the boys.

Our parents were still out front and, needless to say, they didn't notice we were running away. We went out the back door, and George climbed over the fence. Butch lifted me over and then joined us on the other side. We cut through the neighbor's back yard, and then we ran for what seemed like a mile, even if it was only a couple of blocks. Though we lived in the city, there were no street lights on our block so I cried because I was scared of the dark. Finally, George let go of my arm and said, "Fine, go back home, but you're going alone." He ran to catch up with Butch. I stood there for just a moment, looking at my brothers run away from me. Should I follow them? Instead, I turned around and ran as fast as I could towards home. As I neared the front yard, I could still hear them arguing. I slowly walked into the front yard. Instead of asking where I had been, Mama yanked me up by the arm and told Daddy that he would never see me again. She said that she was going to take me away and she cursed him again. Of us three kids, I was Daddy's only biological child; my brothers had a different father. Daddy grabbed me by my other arm, pulled me to his side, and shouted back at Mama. I was in the middle of a tug-of-war. Back and forth my body was jerked, sometimes pulling my arms and sometimes my hair. I tuned out all the words. I felt like I was going to pass out. There was a lot of pain, and I cried. I cried because of the physical pain and the agony I felt deep inside. I loved Mama and Daddy very much, and I didn't want to lose either one of them. I wanted to be with them both. There was nothing I could do but let them fight over me. My body was being pulled and my heart was breaking into pieces, so I screamed out for help.

Maybe the boys heard my scream, or maybe they were worried about me, or maybe they were afraid too, but whatever the cause, they came back to the house. Somehow they pulled me out of the battle. Mama shoved us three kids into the house and told us to stay there. I ran in and hid behind the lazy boy chair that faced the living room. The screen door slammed as Mama went outside. Seconds later, Mama came running back into the house. I'll never forget her words, half out of breath, as she made her way into the kitchen and yanked open the drawer that we called the knife drawer. "I'm going to kill that son of a bitch! I'm going to kill him!"

Oh, my God! My Daddy! I jumped up from my hiding spot and darted out the front door. I heard the screen door slam behind me.

Daddy was running in the road and was only a house or two away. He was a very big man: 6'7" tall, about 275 pounds with huge, size 16 feet. He wasn't very fast. I screamed, "Daddy" several times, and he finally stopped and turned towards me. He waited for me, and, when I reached him, he quickly scooped me up in his big arms and held me tightly. He was dripping with sweat and his clothes smelled like smoke. His voice was slurred and trembling as he told me he was going to take me away. The screen door slammed again. He turned away from home and began to run with me in his arms. I looked back and saw Mama in the shadows of the house. I was confused and I began to cry. Oh no, where are we going? My Mama, my brothers, my toys- everything was back there- at <u>home</u>. I thought to myself, "Please, Daddy don't take me away from here. Let's go home, and it'll all be okay. Please don't take me away." Daddy cradled me in his arms and continued to run. As he ran, he repeated over and over that he wanted us to go away. He wanted us to be happy. Standing outside the house, Mama began to scream, "My baby, my baby, my baby!" I could feel my clothes absorbing the moisture from my Daddy's perspiration, I began to shiver, then I yelled out, "Mommy! Mommy!"

She ran towards us, and, as I continued to scream to her, Daddy slowly came to a stop. His tight hold on me began to loosen as he put me back down on the ground. I felt so much pain when I looked up and saw my Daddy's face. For the first time in my young life, I saw tears rolling down his cheeks. With my heart pounding out of my chest, I looked up to him to say, "I love you Daddy," but, he never heard my words. Mama ran up behind Daddy and shouted "You son of a b-tch!" Out of the darkness, I saw the knife. It was the butcher knife from the kitchen drawer.

I stood there in terror as I heard Daddy let out a piercing cry. I watched his face. His mouth was stretched wide, and his body became rigid with pain. Mama had ripped open Daddy's back with the butcher knife. He was cut wide open from his left shoulder to his right hip. Daddy dropped face down to the ground. His shirt was sliced open and I could see the blood spilling out. Mama turned to me and screamed in a scary deep voice, "Get into the house!" I stood there terrified, trying to understand what was happening. I stood there until someone grabbed me and started running back towards home.

2
The Next Day

The last thing I remember about Daddy being stabbed was riding in the back seat of the police car with George. Mama rode in the front of the car and Butch rode in the ambulance with Daddy. He was in the hospital for quite a while. I found out later that Daddy had 186 stitches in his back but he was going to be okay.

Mama stayed in bed most of the next day. We tiptoed around the house, whispering and trying not to wake her up. I played quietly in the living room and then went out to the back yard. It was a boring day until the phone rang. Butch called me into the house. He said that Lisa's mom called and wanted to know if I would like to go over and play. Lisa Price and I were the same age. She lived just a couple of houses down the road. Butch said that I would have to ask Mama...myself.

Cautiously, I opened the door to our bedroom. As I stepped inside, I turned around and shut the door quietly. The heavy dark curtains were closed. With the door shut, it was very dark in the room. I waited a few seconds for my eyes to adjust. Mama was on her side facing the wall with her back to me. I couldn't see her face or her hands. Mama was always mad when someone woke her up, so I quietly tiptoed over to her bed. I paused just a moment before I whispered, "Mama, can I please go to Lisa's house for a little bit?" Startling me, she rolled over towards me, "You already woke me up, when you opened the door, you little brat. I don't care just get out of here, but you better be back in one hour and don't you dare say anything about your father!" I knew I needed to get out of there fast before she could get out of bed or change her mind, so I turned around and scurried out of the bedroom. I whispered, "Thank you," as I softly shut the door.

I walked along the curb to Lisa's house with my head down. I was balancing on the curb as if it were a beam. Suddenly, I noticed something just up ahead of me. It was dried blood on the curb and road. I couldn't stand to look at it. I was trying to forget the entire night. Poor Daddy. I hated to remember the tears he had in his eyes, the disappointment he had in me, and I couldn't bear to think about it! Even though Mama had warned me not to cross our neighbor's yard, I backed away from the street and ran across the grass.

Lisa's house was quiet because she was an only child. She had her own room and it was full of toys. Lisa got to pick out the color of her walls. They were soft pink. Playing at Lisa's was always fun. Mrs. Price seemed to be the "perfect" mom. She was always kind to me and never raised her voice to Lisa while I visited. Lisa invited me into her house, and we sat on the couch for a moment while her mom got us a glass of iced tea. I thought it was odd that we didn't just go to Lisa's room to play, but I sat there waiting for her mom to return. When she did, she asked me several questions. "What happened last night?" she asked in a soft voice. "Nothing." I replied. "Are you okay?" she inquired. I said, "Yes Ma'am." She asked me, "What was all that noise last night, and why did the police come?" I told her that I couldn't talk about it to anyone. I told her that if I did, I would get into big trouble. Mrs. Price then told me that she understood, and that I didn't have to tell her anything. She took a sip of tea and said she had a good idea. She said that I could tell her tape recorder what happened, and that way my Mom wouldn't be mad at me. A tape recorder isn't a person, so it would be okay. I wanted to talk to the tape recorder. We didn't have one, and I thought it would be fun. So I told Mrs. Price that I would tell the tape recorder what happened to Daddy.

As I waited in the living room for Mrs. Price to come in with the recorder, I remember looking around the room and thinking that their house was similar to our house. They had the same two bedrooms, one living room and one kitchen. The biggest difference was that they had wall to wall carpet and a lot of pictures of their family on the wall.

Mrs. Price entered the room from the hallway and set the recorder down on the end table next to me. Lisa was sitting on the other side. Mrs. Price got everything ready and then showed me where I was supposed to talk into. She would hit the buttons on the recorder for me. I didn't really know what to say, so Mrs. Price prompted me with a few questions; "Cheri, can you tell the recorder why the police came last night? Why were your parents fighting?" We didn't get too far when I heard someone knock at the door. I had forgotten to mention to Lisa's mom that I could only stay for one hour. As I heard the knock, my heart raced, I hoped it wasn't Mama at the door. I was relieved to see that it was my brother, George. He had come to get me. I asked him if my hour was up, and he just glared at me. Once we got outside and we were heading home, he told me the news, "You're in trouble. Mama is mad, and she's gonna beat you."

"Am I late? Am I late?" I asked repeatedly, but he wouldn't tell me. I started to cry before I even walked into the house because I knew what I was walking into. The minute I saw Mama's face, I knew she was really mad. Her hair, after being slept on, was ratted and made Mama look as though she had placed her finger in the light socket. Her small, squinty, green eyes were filled with an evil threatening aura, and her voice was harsh and bitter. There was terror in my voice when I yelled out, "I'm sorry, I forgot to tell her what time I had to be home!" I started begging over and over, "I'm sorry, I'm sorry, please don't hit me Mama, please!" That's when I saw her swing her arm back and WHAM! The blast hit me on the side of the head. I fell down on the floor and lay there for a second. My face was burning where her hand caught my cheek.

"I told you not to tell anyone! How many times do I have to tell you something?! Stop crying!" Mama yelled. I tried to stand up and she kicked me. Butch and George had quietly left the room. They had endured many beatings in their lifetime and knew they couldn't say a word.

I wanted to tell her so badly that I hadn't disobeyed. I had only told the recorder. Instead, I lay on the floor and hid my face until I finally got up and ran into my room, slammed the door, jumped into my bed and covered up with all my stuffed animals. In that safety, I quickly started praying, "Please don't come in, please don't come in, please..." until I drifted off to sleep.

To this day, I don't know how Mama found out about what went on at Lisa's house. Mama may have sent one of the boys over to "check on me" and, when prompted by Mama, they felt compelled to tell her the truth about what they saw or heard. I only know now that it doesn't matter how she found out. Asking my brothers if they "tattled" on me would only bring more pain for both them and for me. My brothers had protected me many times, and it seemed that this one time, they were unable to shield me from the darkness of abuse. I am sure that their pain was as great as mine.

3
The Good Side of Mama

One autumn afternoon, Mama gave me a cat. She was orange, black, and white and not even a year old. Mama told me that she was a "Calico" because she had three colors. So, that's what I named her: Calico. I loved that cat. She cuddled with me all the time. When I went to bed she would snuggle right up on top of my pillow. Sometimes, when Mama and Daddy would fight, I would get scared and curl up in a little ball with Calico. She would purr and it would always make me feel better.

Daddy didn't like cats. He told us that when he was a boy on the farm, he would find a baby kitten and tie it to the railroad tracks. After the train ran over the poor helpless kitten, he would use its remains for fishing bait. My brothers said that Daddy was pulling my leg, but I still kept Calico away from him.

4
A Real Surprise, Age 4

When Spring came, Calico started getting fat and Mama explained to me that she was going to have baby kittens. Mama and I decided to make a bed outside under the carport where Calico could have her kittens. We walked two blocks up to the Little General. Mama and I cut across a field, where people dumped their old furniture and trash. We were careful not to step on any glass.

I liked going to the Little General. My grandma (Mama's mother) would stop by and see our family then take me up to the Little General to get an icy or a coke. It was a real treat for me and made me feel special, as she would take just me. Grandma only lived about five blocks from our house. Even though we lived close enough to walk to her house, we never did. Mama called our neighborhood the bad part of town. There was lots of crime.

When Mama and I got to the store, we asked the clerk for a box. She said we could go out back and dig whatever we needed out of the big dumpster, and so we did. Mama got me an icy and then we walked home. Once home, we found an old rug for a bed, and some old bowls for dishes.

Mama said that Calico was going to have her babies any day now. Mama tried to make Calico stay outside so that she would have her kittens in the box. Every morning, bright and early, I would jump out of bed, run outside and check for kittens. Then one day I ran out to check on her, but she wasn't there. She wasn't anywhere to be found. I searched the front and back yard, the neighbor's yard. I searched everywhere but those scary woods. I even looked in the street to see if she had been hit by a car, but thankfully she wasn't there. Mama suggested that I check inside the house. I looked under the couch, under the lazy boy, in the kitchen, and all over. I had just about given up hope when I checked underneath my bed. There she was, lying on her side. With her were five tiny kittens. Somehow she had crawled back into the house and snuggled up under my warm bed.

I got on my belly and scooted under the bed for a closer look. She had five, beautiful kittens: one looked just like her, two black kittens, one orange tabby and one solid white. I decided that I would be nice and share them with my family. I gave one kitten to each person, even Daddy. He couldn't hate a kitten if it was a gift from me!

Softly, I stroked Calico and whispered what a good cat she was. Someone tapped on my leg. I backed myself out from under my bed, sneezing from the dust and saw Mama staring at me. She asked, "What on earth are you doing?"

"Come down and look what Calico did!" was all I could say.

Mama got down on her hands and knees and peeked under the bed. In a soft, happy whisper she said, "I declare."

Mama looked at me and smiled and motioned for me to go into the kitchen with her. She didn't want to wake up Daddy. We went into the kitchen, starting the day off on the right foot, enjoying each other's company.

5
The Car Accident

One day late in May of 1969, Great Grandma Sarasota came over to visit us. She was Mama's grandmother. I had so many grandmas and grandpas that I called them each a different nick name. This one lived in Sarasota, so I called her Grandma Sarasota. Great Grandma Sarasota was my Pop- Pop's mother. (I called my real grandfather Pop-Pop, I also had a step-grandpa) Pop-pop was Mama's Daddy.

Mama's parent's divorced a long time ago. Her Mama moved out to California for a short while, so I called her Grandma California. She remarried seven or eight times and when I was two years old, she finally married a man named Harry. Being a quiet and sweet little man, he became the one I lovingly called Grandpa.

Grandma California's mom was also alive and I called her Grandma Mac. She drove really fast and scared us all to death. Her first husband was killed, but she remarried so I still had a Great Grandpa. Her first husband was stabbed to death in a fight when my Grandma was only five years old. I didn't have any grandparents from my Daddy's side. His Mama died when he was fourteen. She was beheaded in a car accident. His Daddy died when he was sixteen of some type of cancer.

Great Grandma Sarasota couldn't drive anymore so Daddy had to pick her up to bring her over and then take her back home. Mama wanted me to 'keep an eye on Daddy,' so I always had to ride everywhere with him.

Daddy would usually complain about having to run Mama's relatives all over town. However, he didn't complain this time, and I suppose it was because he had a new car.

Daddy had bought a used red convertible from a guy at work. Daddy told me it was just like one he had in high school. I think that's why he liked it so much. Driving to Grandma Sarasota's house, Daddy said that March is the worst time for tourists. Sarasota was about twenty minutes from our house but, because of the traffic, it took us almost an hour to get to her home. The worst part about the trip was that if we took too long, Mama would get upset and ask me a hundred questions when we got home. "Who was your father with?" "Did he meet any women?" "Did you stop at the bar?"

That day, the boys rode with Daddy and me to take Grandma Sarasota home. Daddy was driving fast. I thought that he wanted to drop Grandma off and get home to avoid any unnecessary fighting with Mama. The boys and I tried to talk Daddy into driving with the top down, but Daddy said it was going to rain.

Daddy and Grandma Sarasota sat in the front seat and us kids were in the back. As the youngest, it was always my unfavorable duty to sit in the middle of the boys. I considered the boys blessed to have a window seat. They considered it misery to have a little sister in the seat next to them.

It was fun riding in Daddy's new car, driving fast, and sliding into each one of my brothers as Daddy turned the corners. I was laughing and really bugging the boys when Daddy turned around and said in an irritated voice, "Stop that giggling!"

Then, BOOM! CRASH! Everyone went flying forward. I looked down and saw that my left knee was bleeding, and I started to cry. But no one paid attention to me. I looked at Butch, he was crawling out the two broken windows on the driver's side, and George was trying to squeeze between the front passenger seat and the smashed door. I looked up to see Grandma Sarasota. There was blood all over the dashboard. The front windshield was shattered. I thought she was dead.

Her limp body fell over towards Daddy. I couldn't see her face. The top of her head was full of blood matted hair. I could see glass sticking out of her scalp. Daddy was slumped forward against the steering wheel that was jammed into his ribs. His legs were crushed up into the dashboard.

I sat there and screamed, "Daddy! Daddy! Daddy!" A man ran up to the car out of breath, looked inside and yelled, "Call an ambulance!" George was already at a nearby house asking for help. Butch tried to open Daddy's door. He was yelling for Daddy not to die, "Dad, get up, don't die, Dad we need ya, Dad!" Butch told me to get out of the car and go sit on the curb. I squeezed out of the back between Grandma and the door, and went over to the curb.

I was so terrified! I just sat there, my knees up on the curb, my arms crossed around my legs and my face buried so that I couldn't see anything. I tried to cover my ears, but there was too much noise. Then I heard George screaming at Butch, "Someone's coming to help!"

A man came running out of his house towards our car. He wasn't as old as Daddy, but he looked as tall as my Daddy. He was very thin. He ran over to the car and told everyone to back away. I couldn't see what he was doing. In the next few minutes, I heard the creaking sound of bending metal as this guy yanked open the car door that no one else could open. Then he pulled Daddy from the car, and ran with Daddy in his arms past me. I jumped up and tried to run with them, but George stopped me. Butch was running around telling everyone, "Do something!" Then two ambulances and a police car arrived.

Daddy, Grandma, and Butch were all taken to the emergency room. Grandma and Daddy were rushed into surgery and Butch was admitted for shock. The police called Mama and she came to the hospital. I was told that it was a miracle that Grandma and Daddy survived the accident. They spent a great deal of time in the hospital. Butch was okay and was released the same day.

After the accident I often wondered who the man was that saved Daddy's life. It was so miraculous how he carried Daddy in his arms. I now know that God sends angels from Heaven to watch and guard over us, and just perhaps that man was an angel sent from God.

6
Mama's Boyfriend

The doctor said that Daddy was very lucky. After his surgery he walked on crutches for a long time. During most of that time, Daddy stayed home from work. When he did go back to work he found out that he was being transferred to another job sight. Though the transfer was only for a few months. They wanted him to be a supervisor for the welders and that was a promotion for him. He was being transferred to Plant City, a town three hours from Bradenton. Since his job was only going to be there for six months, Daddy decided to live there during the week and come home on the weekends. At first, when Daddy said that he was moving to another city, I thought it was because of the way he and Mama fought. Since they fought over me all the time, I also thought it might have been my fault he was leaving.

As in everything, there were good days and bad days while Daddy was away. Mama would sometimes work about the house singing the old southern songs, and hymns that Grandma Sarasota had taught her. Then there were other days that weren't so good.

As time went on, the good days became fewer and the bad days more frequent. Mama was going out to the bar more now that Daddy wasn't home. Many times we would stop at Josie's Bar and Grill during the day when my brothers were at school. Mama, Grandma California and my Grandpa would all stay at the bar most of the day. Mama knew the bartender, his name was Willis. He was a friend of Pop-Pop's. He looked like he was a hundred years old. He had gray hair and his skin was dark and wrinkled from the sun, but he was always pretty nice. Sometimes, after the bar closed, we would go over to his house. I was warned to never tell Daddy about going to Willis' house.

7
The Motel

Ray's Bar and Grill was another place where Mama and my grandparents hung out to drink and socialize. Ray's Bar and Grill was on the corner in Samoset. It was an old, gray, wooden shack that looked like it was going to fall apart. The same people went there every day, and we knew each of them by name.

Mama met a man. His name was Pat. He was younger than Mama. He was thin and of medium height. He had dark brown short hair, and he was very soft spoken. He smiled a lot and he was cordial to me. There were times when it seemed that Pat protected me. He didn't come right out and defend me, but, in a strange way, he sort of protected me. Often, when Mama was really mad, either yelling or hitting me, I would pray to Jesus. I would pray that He would make Mama stop whatever she was doing. It was at those times that Pat always seemed to call or just show up at the house. I used to think it was a miracle that Pat showed up at just the right time. Now I know that miracles are just an answered prayer from God. I really liked Pat. Though he was not my Daddy, I was glad that he was in Mama's life.

One hot summer day in June, Pat took Mama, the boys, and me to a motel to stay overnight. I was excited on the way to the motel. Pat promised to take us to a motel with a pool and it all sounded fun to me. But before going to the motel, we stopped for a beer. Before going anywhere, it seemed we had to stop for beer. Mama and Pat loaded the cooler full of beer and cokes (we referred to all soft drinks as "cokes") then we were off to Sarasota. Finally, we found a motel. Pat went in and got our room, and I was surprised that my brothers and I stayed in one room all by ourselves while my Mama and Pat stayed in the room next door.

It was late afternoon when we finally got up to our rooms. Mama and Pat had a big bed, and it had a machine on it that made it wiggle. There was a door that connected Mama's room with our room. Mama locked it and said that we would have to use the outside door. She didn't want anyone just "walking right in."

Our room had two smaller beds. The boys said they each got a bed, and neither one wanted to sleep with me. I didn't care where I slept, all I wanted to do was to go swimming. Butch and George didn't want to go with me. They were mad about coming to the motel and wanted to just stay in and pout. Mama and Pat said they would take me in a little bit. I argued that it would be too late, but Mama insisted that she and Pat would take me later. Mama turned on the television and said she would be in to get me in a little while.

As I waited for Mama, I sat on the end of the bed in my swimsuit and watched television. Butch and George, didn't like "Mama messing around on Dad," and they weren't excited about this spur of the moment decision to go stay in a "cheap motel." They didn't like Pat as much as I did.

I watched one television show and then another and finally I couldn't wait any longer. I decided to knock on the adjacent door. Mama and Pat didn't answer. I knocked louder. "Mama, when are we going swimmin'?" No one answered me. Butch said that they were probably busy or in the shower. I sat down to watch television again. It was already getting dark outside. I cried to Butch about being hungry but there wasn't anything he could do. A little later Pat came over and asked if we wanted Kentucky Fried Chicken® for dinner. He was going out to get dinner, more beer and cokes. Then Pat looked at me, "Oh, we were going to go swimming,

38

weren't we?" Now that it was dark, it was too late to go, so he promised to take me in the morning. The night was long. Our motel was right next to a noisy highway and I was scared. I wanted to be home with my stuffed animals. I prayed that tomorrow would come quickly as I laid down on George's bed and fell asleep still wearing my bathing suit.

The next morning came and I was ready to go swimming. Butch said, "I betcha Mama doesn't let you go." Immediately, I yelled back at him, "Oh yes she will because Pat promised me!" I ran over and knocked on the adjacent door. Again there was no answer, "Mama! Mama! Let's go swimmin'! Mama!" Then Mama yelled back, "<u>Please</u> be quiet! I don't feel good!" Pat came to the door. Sympathetically, he said, "You better get ready to go, your Mom is sick." I was so disappointed.

When Pat turned the corner to take us home, he was surprised to see that Daddy's car was under the carport. Daddy had decided to come home a day early to surprise us. Pat pulled up in front of the house and Mama told us to get out of the car. I could hear the screech of Pat's tires as he drove away.

When we got into the house, Mama ran straight to the bathroom and threw up. She locked herself in and she wouldn't open the door for Daddy. Daddy sat on the end of his bed and asked the boys and me a lot of questions. He wanted to know who we were with and where we were. The boys wouldn't answer him. They knew that Mama would be mad if they told. Daddy gently pulled me by my arm over to the bed. Daddy said that everything would be okay if I just told him who Mama spent the night with. I started to tell Daddy how we couldn't go swimming. Just then, Mama came running out of the bathroom and into the room. Butch and George told me to shut up. Mama pushed the boys out of the way and came over to the bed. Mama tried to grab me away from Daddy, but Daddy had a tight grip on my arm. Daddy stood up and pushed Mama down on the ground. She and I both started crying. Mama was pleading for me not to say anything to Daddy. I was pleading to them to please stop fighting. Daddy was asking me over and over, "What's his name?" Here I was again, being torn between the two people I loved the most in the entire world. I was just too afraid to tell Daddy, and when I wouldn't say anything, he finally got mad and left the room. I felt so torn between the two of them. Who was I suppose to obey?

8
Without a Good-bye

Mama promised Daddy that she would never see Pat again. She kept her promise until one day right before the boys went back to school, something terrible happened. The kittens were now big enough to run around on their own. Most of the time they stayed outside under the carport.

We had borrowed Grandma Mac's car while Daddy was away at work. We decided to spend the whole day at the beach one last time before school started . We had gotten everything together and then it was my job to make sure the kittens weren't underneath the wheels before we backed out of the driveway. We loaded up the trunk, and I ran around the car quickly glancing underneath to check for kittens. It looked clear so I jumped in and Mama started the car. She put it in reverse and pressed on the gas. Immediately we heard the awful sound of one of the kittens getting crushed by the tire.

"Oh, Cheri!" Mama said, as she turned off the car and told Butch to get out and see what we had just run over. Butch came up to the window and said we had just crushed the little black kitten that I had given to Mama. She was particularly attached to that kitten. She told the boys to take me into the house and not let me see the kitten. Then Mama came in crying and called Pat. She asked him if he would come over and help her bury it. Pat came over and buried the little, black kitten in the woods across the street. Then he and Mama went out for a beer and the boys and I stayed at home.

When Daddy got home that weekend, I was at my cousin Tommie Lee's house. She was only six weeks younger than me and we spent a lot of time together.

Daddy somehow found out that Pat had come over and he was furious. When I came home from Tommie Lee's house, I noticed that there was something different. There were no kittens in the yard or under the carport. I ran into the house calling for Calico but she wasn't anywhere to be found. The boys were the only ones home so I busted into their room demanding to know where my cats were. They told me that Daddy got mad and took them to the Humane Society. I didn't even get the chance to say good-bye. The boys also told me that Daddy had other bad news for us too. We were all moving to Homestead, Florida. It was about five hours away. Daddy's job in Plant City was suppose to be ending in December. Daddy and his crew finished the job early and instead of coming back to Bradenton, his company, Mid-Valley® wanted him to move to another job sight in Homestead. We had to sell our house right away and move.

9
Homestead, Florida

The move wasn't as bad as I thought it would be. The house we moved into was much bigger than our old house, but it needed a lot of work. Most of the screens were torn, some of the windows were broken, and the inside was filthy. On the other hand, this house had a swimming pool, and I had my own room. Even though the pool was in terrible condition, I was still excited to have it. The little water left in the bottom of the pool was greenish blue. Mama explained that it was full of algae. Floating on top of the water was little slimy circles with black dots. Mama said that frogs had crawled in the holes of the screen that surrounded the porch and laid eggs in the pool. Daddy said he could patch the holes.

The house belonged to a man that my Daddy worked with at Mid-Valley®. The man was transferred and couldn't sell the house, so he rented it to us. Even Butch and George liked it. There was a cool place for them to ride their bikes right down the road. We had neighbors on each side of us, but across the street and down the road it was just fields full of the sharp two-edged saw grass.

Scrubbing the algae off the sides of the pool turned out to be quite a job, especially for George because he kept accidentally falling in. Butch thought that was hilarious. Daddy never <u>did</u> get around to fixing the holes in the screen. So, every morning my brothers and I had to go out and catch frogs in the pool. I thought it was fun to watch the boys swim around trying to catch the frogs. It was my job to walk around the pool and use the net to scoop up the freshly laid tadpole eggs.

10
Preschool

Preschool. My brothers said that school was the worst thing since liver, but I didn't think it was all that bad. My teacher was very nice and paid a lot of attention to me. We learned the alphabet song, the teapot song and we colored a lot. Every day Mama would drop me off at school. Later she would come and pick me up. There weren't too many kids in my class, and it seemed like I had a lot of friends. Everything seemed to be going good, until Daddy came home from work one day and told us that he was getting transferred <u>again</u>. Daddy's job was working for a construction company that built boilers for power plants. Whenever the job was finished, they would send him on to the next plant. The boys were mad. They wanted to stay. Butch and George had met a few friends. Daddy said that his job would be finished by the end of the year and we would be moving before Christmas.

11
Bradenton, Florida

We moved back to Bradenton in December of 1969. We had to rent a place until Daddy found out where he was going to be transferred. We drove by our old house, and they were cutting down the woods across the street. Daddy said that they were going to put up apartment buildings for colored people and that we moved out just in time. As much as I disliked those woods, it was sad to see the trees cut down.

Daddy was laid off until they found a place to transfer him. He said that we didn't have much money, and that's why we had to rent this old, run-down, wooden shack. Mama said that Daddy was just being cheap. This place was the smallest house we had ever lived in. It only had one bedroom, and the bathroom didn't work so well. Sometimes we would have to go out back and use an old toilet in the shed. Mama and Daddy slept in the bedroom. I slept on the couch and the boys slept on the back porch. The porch was the worst because the floor sloped downward and wasn't very comfortable for sleeping. Mama tried to make the best of things and let me play outside a lot with the other kids in the neighborhood. It seemed as though I spent all my time playing outside in the dirt.

Light Beyond the Darkness

12
The Boy's Rug

I started kindergarten. I went to the same school that Mama and brothers went to when they were little. I thought it would be fun, but the teacher didn't seem to like me much.

One day at nap time, I put my head down on the little bumpy rug that Mama had given me. It was thin and not very comfortable but it was all we could afford so I appreciated it. As I lay there, I noticed that the boy next to me had the most beautiful rug that I had ever seen. It was thicker and longer than my rug. It wasn't as colorful but it had specks of pure white, silver and a deep purple. The best part about his rug was that it had long, white tassels that floated from each end of the rug. More than anything I wanted his rug. I touched the tassels, petting them and smoothing them out with my fingers. The boy noticed me touching "his" rug and got mad. He whispered for me to stop, but I couldn't. Every time he laid his head down, I reached over and smoothed and touched another tassel, dreaming that it was my rug, warm and snugly. I was thinking that if I had a beautiful and soft rug like that, I could go to sleep during nap time. The boy lifted his head and saw me touch another tassel. He jumped up and ran over to the teacher. Everyone looked at me as he tattled to the teacher. The teacher, without getting out of her chair, warned me that I had better stop picking on the boy's rug. I couldn't stop. This time when the boy lay down, just to spite him, I started smoothing out all the tassels. The boy jumped up again and ran over to the teacher to tattle once again. The teacher called me over to her desk, gave me a stern look, and told me that she had already warned me. She opened her center drawer and took out an oval shaped paddle. The teacher told me to lean over her chair and she then spanked my bottom with the paddle. WAP! WAP! With every sting I screamed a little louder. She said that she would continue to slap my bottom until I quit screaming. Eventually, I got the picture. When the last stinging blow was finished, I was told to go to my rug and stay there while the rest of the class was released from nap to play.

13
Sanford, Florida

Daddy finally got his job back and was transferred again. This time it was a town in Northern Florida called Sanford. Though I didn't like the living conditions of our last house in Bradenton, I did like living close to my cousins and Grandma California. So, I wasn't excited to move.

Our new house seemed okay and there were a few kids my age in the neighborhood. We rented our new house. It was a reddish brown house with red shutters and trim. It had a similar layout to our old house in Bradenton where I shared a bedroom with Mama and Daddy, but this house was flipped around. This house had the carport on the right and the bedrooms on the left. Near the carport was our front door. Our living room had one window. Unlike our old house, this one had a dining room. It was small, but there was a window right above our dinner table. Between our table and the kitchen there was a door leading to the back yard. The door had many narrow panes of glass in it. It rattled and sounded like it was going to break if it was shut too hard. There was a long hallway that connected the living room to the bedrooms. My bedroom was the first on the left. Then we had a laundry closet. That's where Mama threw all the clean clothes that we kids needed to iron and fold. Our parents' room was next, and, finally, my brothers' room was across from Mama's and Daddy's. The floors weren't carpeted, but Mama found some really nice throw rugs to place throughout the house. Mama loved to shop at the Salvation Army® and Goodwill®. She could find the best merchandise for the lowest price. For me it was like shopping for a treasure.

Our new back yard was very big. This time we had neighbors on each side and across the street. Behind our house were woods. The woods separated our block from the highway and helped keep the noise down. Butch and George said that we always lived around woods so that Mama and Daddy wouldn't have to worry about the neighbors hearing and complaining about them fighting so much.

14
The Good Life

Life in Sanford started out much different from Bradenton. We moved in June and right away, Daddy put up a jungle gym in the back yard for me. It was brand new and he said it was my belated birthday present! I really loved it! I would climb all the way to the top and pretend to be an acrobat. Sometimes, I even pretended to be a monkey.

Mama decided to study for her high school diploma (GED). She decided that she wanted to go to nursing school to be an LPN.

Mama also met a Welcome Wagon lady and decided to join a Baptist Church. She talked Daddy into going to church too. We went almost every Sunday. I loved going to church and listening to the beautiful piano music, and seeing Mama's face light up as she sang the hymns. Mama had a beautiful voice and I loved to hear her sing the gospel.

This church didn't believe in drinking, smoking, dancing or any music that didn't declare the gospel. Mama and Daddy pretended that they weren't smokers, and they even stopped going to bars for a while. Mama poured all the booze down the drain and tried to quit smoking, but quitting made her easily agitated.

The only downfall to Sanford was that the closest beach, New Smyrna, was a little over an hour away. The boys, Mama, and I all loved going to the beach. Almost every weekend Mama would take us to the beach, if we cleaned the house for her.

Light Beyond the Darkness

15
A Part of Mama I Loved

Mama was born and raised in Florida. After a few drinks in a bar, Mama would often speak in a soft sweet voice, with an unusual French sounding accent and a trace of her southern upbringing. It was an unusual combination but it was her trademark. It seemed as though the men liked it. In the bar, she would treat us kids great, like a very loving mom. After the bar, she would turn 180 degrees. Her voice became angry and scary. It was rough and often spurred out vulgar language. In that temperament, we all feared her. To us, she seemed like the devil, and we didn't put anything past her. But there was another side to Mama; a good side of Mama. She loved church, and she loved God. Deep inside her heart, Mama wanted to please God. Sometimes she would walk around the house (usually when she wasn't under the influence of alcohol) singing great hymns that Grandma Sarasota had sung to her years before. It was in those moods that Mama taught me all about Jesus. She told me that I should pray to Him all the time. I knew that Jesus held a special place in Mama's heart and when she followed Him, her kindness, and gentle spirit emanated like never before. That was the Mama that I loved so dearly, and later in my life respected and wanted to know even better.

Light Beyond the Darkness

16
Broken Promises

Mama often made promises to take us places if we cleaned the house. As a result, we were able to go to Disney World a couple times, and even spent vacations in a hotel on the beach. On one particular day in July, Mama promised to take us to the beach the following day if, of course, we held up on our side of the bargain. The next day Mama woke up on the wrong side of the bed. She found a hundred things wrong with the house the boys and I had cleaned the day before. If we wanted to go to the beach, we had to finish cleaning while she took Daddy to work. The boys and I cleaned fast and hard after Mama left. When she returned, she found a couple more things for the boys to do while she and I made sandwiches. Finally, around 11:00a.m. we were ready to go.

It was a hot and humid day. Mama didn't want to turn on the air conditioner in the car because it used too much gas. Butch, George and I were all complaining about the heat and our late start to the beach. She said that we were driving her crazy with all of our complaining. From the front seat, Mama overheard Butch say something about how Mama woke up in a bad mood because she didn't have a cigarette. She had quit smoking just a couple days before. That made Mama angry, and she told Butch, "Well, at the next place I'll stop to buy a pack, if that's what you want." Softly, Butch spoke back, "Fine with me." Mama stopped at a gas station. When she got back to the car I saw that she had bought a beer but not any cigarettes. Mama said that the gas station didn't have the right brand so she would have to stop at another store. She passed a Seven-Eleven® and didn't stop. The boys looked at each other in confusion, surely the Seven- Eleven would have the brand of cigarettes that she wanted. Then without Mama saying a word we knew where we were going- to the next bar.

The next bar wasn't as far as we had anticipated. It was just up the road from the Seven-Eleven. I had never noticed it before but Mama had driven that road many times. As we pulled in Mama told us to sit in the car and wait.

We were use to waiting but somehow, it never got any easier. Even with all the doors open, our white four-door Ford, parked in the sun, was boiling hot. I stripped down to my bathing suit, and the boys took off their shirts. The sweat still continued to roll down our faces. We waited for over an hour and a half before the boys finally sent me, barefoot, bathing suit and all, into the bar to see what was going on.

Mama was sitting at the bar with some man, smoking a cigarette and drinking a beer. "Mama," I asked, "Aren't we going to the beach?" She answered back in a sweet voice, "In a little bit. Why don't you go tell the boys to come in and play some pool?" When I told the boys what Mama said, their reply was "Don't plan on going to the beach, Cheri. We have to be home to pick up Dad at 5:00 p.m." It was already getting late. Butch got some cokes and sandwiches out of the cooler and we sat outside behind the bar in the shade. We sat on our beach towels, talked about Mama and ate our late lunch.

After our sandwiches, Mama still wasn't ready to go, so the boys threw the football around, and I ran around looking for things to do. I wandered off to an old shed and pretended to be kidnapped. It was fun until I heard Mama hollering my name. This time it wasn't in that same, sweet voice she was using inside. Immediately,

I took off running, looking up to see where she was standing. I didn't even see the old rusty rake that was lying upside down in the ankle high grass. Suddenly, I felt a sharp puncture as one of the prongs entered the ball of my foot between my first and second toe. OUCH! Limping back to the car, I saw Butch and George shaking their heads at me. Mama came running towards me screaming, "Where were you? Don't you know we have to pick up your father?!" She was even more mad when she saw my foot. "Now look what you've done! Your father's going to kill me!" Mama took me to the hospital, and I had to get a tetanus shot.

Light Beyond the Darkness

17
Stitches, This Time in the Head

Sundays were my favorite days. We often did something as a family. Sometimes after church we would go out to eat. Sometimes we'd go canepole fishing off the sea wall. I liked to do things after church because Mama was always in a good mood. Mama said that Sunday was the day to ask the Lord to forgive you for what you did wrong and then to ask him to help you to do what is right. There were many Sundays that Mama tried to start over. Sometimes starting over meant pouring all the booze down the drain, <u>again</u>. It meant being a more Christ-like woman. Starting over sometimes meant being a better listener, less temperamental, kinder to Daddy and us kids. Sometimes it would last a day. Sometimes a few days, and occasionally, it would last a week. Daddy didn't seem to like church much. He said that he believed in God, but he thought that most of the people in church were hypocrites.

More often than not, Daddy fell asleep in church. I don't know how Daddy could fall asleep during our preacher's sermon. Our preacher was loud. He would bang on the pulpit and shout "AMEN" and then you'd hear the congregation shout back, "Amen." I would look over at Daddy only to see his head quickly lift off his chest and then slowly drift back down, never fully awaking to the celebration of our preacher's sermon. The real problem with Daddy falling asleep in church was that he snored like a bulldozer. Mama would nudge him with her elbow and then you'd see Daddy's chin jolt up again and with a stern look from Mama you can bet he tried his best to stay awake.

Even though Sundays helped Mama to start over, it seemed like the change never lasted long enough for me. Our life was a never-ending circle. Mama would try to change, but then Daddy would stop and have a drink after work. When Daddy came home late, he would lie and say that he worked overtime, but Mama would always smell his breath. Mama didn't trust Daddy at all, and if Mama smelled a trace of alcohol on Daddy's breath, then there would be a fight. Mama would always accuse Daddy of cheating on her. In order to pay Daddy back, Mama would then go out drinking and sometimes even meet a man. But I guess Mama didn't like the circle any better than us kids, because she was always trying to start over.

One humid August afternoon in 1971, Daddy got home late, and dinner got cold as we waited. Mama ate in silence as Daddy tried to tell us about his day and make a few jokes. He would always make up something funny to tell us during dinner. After dinner, Mama said she wanted to talk to Daddy alone, but Daddy said he had to go to the store to get some milk for tomorrow's breakfast. Mama was mad but she was willing to wait. We all knew that Daddy was trying to postpone his punishment for getting home late. Daddy was gone for hours. In fact, he wasn't even home when it was time for me to go to bed. Mama couldn't hold in the anger any longer and found a bottle of liquor and started to drink. She had tried so hard to keep her promise from the previous Sunday. Now all she could say was, "If that son-of-a-bit-h is going to get drunk, I might as well get drunk, too."

After Mama put me to bed and listened to my prayers, I lay there with my door cracked and my eyes open, waiting for Daddy to come home. Finally, I drifted off into a light sleep. I awoke when I heard Daddy's car turn into the driveway. He had turned off his lights before he even pulled into the yard. Daddy was probably trying to be careful. I lay in my bed listening. Mama must have fallen asleep on the couch. I could hear the "off the air" static of the television buzzing in the background. When my window was open, I could hear everything. Daddy slowly shut his car door and moved towards the locked front door. He fumbled for his keys. Daddy had so many keys on his key ring that it barely fit in his pocket. I always loved to pick a key and ask him, "What's this one for, Daddy?" I would do it about seven or eight times before he would tell me "That's enough."

Daddy's shoes made a light tapping sound as they silently crossed the uncarpeted part of our living room floor. I sat up in bed hoping that Daddy could make it back to his room before Mama woke up. I knew that if Mama woke up, then there would be one heck of a fight.

"You son of a bit-h!" I heard Mama scream as if she had never been asleep at all. I heard her jump up from the couch. At the same time, I jumped up from my bed, threw open my door, and ran out and peeked around the corner. In the few seconds it took me to get to my viewing spot, Mama was up and moving fast. I could see her figure by the light of the television. She had picked up a broom that laid beside the couch, and suddenly swung it at Daddy. I gasped as it cracked him in the side of the head and broke in half. Daddy collapsed on the floor. Mama kicked Daddy in the side, "Get up!" As if she were possessed by a demon, she screamed and kicked hysterically, "Get Up!" Scared of what I saw coming from Mama, I ran back to the boys' room, slammed open the door and cried, "Help!" The boys were already sitting up in bed. They had been awakened by the fight. We all ran out to the living room and Butch calmed Mama down while George ran and got towels to wipe the blood off Daddy's face.
George helped Daddy up and rode with them as Mama drove to the hospital. Daddy came home that night with stitches, this time in his head.

18
Learning to Ride

For Christmas Santa brought me a bike! It had training wheels on it, and I was allowed to ride it in the street in front of my house. Daddy said that he would help me ride without my training wheels someday when he had the time.

One day, I put on my bell-bottomed pants, unmatched socks, long-sleeved shirt and shoes and went out to ride my bike. Butch was sitting outside and saw me get my bike. He walked over and told me to tuck my pants leg into my sock; otherwise, it would get caught in the chain and I would fall. I was embarrassed and felt silly having training wheels at my age. There was a boy down the street younger than me, and he didn't ride with training wheels anymore! Butch understood how I felt and said that if I tucked in my pants, he would teach me how to ride my bike. Without hesitation, I bent over and tucked in my bell-bottoms. Butch ran into the house and found a tool to take off my training wheels and off we went to practice. He ran beside me while I pedaled as hard as I could up and down the road. He was patient with me as he jogged beside the bike muttering over and over, "Pedal, pedal, come on, keep pedaling." I tried and tried to go on my own. Then, finally, Butch was running faster, "Pedal! Pedal, okay you're on your own!" He shouted as he continued to run beside me. He hollered mostly out of breath, "Keep pedaling! You're doing it!" I was so proud of myself. Thanks to Butch, it was one of the best days of my life!

19
Guest for Dinner

When I was seven years old, we had a strange guest join us at dinner time. Some nights we sat at the kitchen table for dinner, other nights we sat in front of the television. Daddy sat at the head of the table and going clockwise it was Mama, Butch, George, and finally on the other side of Daddy, there was my seat. Every time we sat down to eat together we sat in the same positions. The window at the end of the table had several rectangular glass panes in it. There was a screen on the inside so that bugs couldn't get into our house. On the outside of the window there
was a small ledge.

I had two girlfriends who lived near our house. Yolanda lived down the street to the right of our house. Mary lived just a few houses down to the left on the corner. Mary's cat had kittens just a few months earlier. Her Daddy made her keep the kittens outside. They would run under their house and play, and usually they would come out when I went over to visit. They were adorable. I was playing with a couple of the kittens one day when Mama called me home for dinner. I jumped on my bike and pedaled home. In the kitchen, I washed my hands and helped Mama put the food on the table. The boys and Daddy washed up for dinner, too. We sat down and Mama told Daddy to say the grace. As he started, I heard our strange new guest out on the window ledge. It was a short, quiet "Meow." I peeked open my eyes (as did everyone else), and there on the ledge of the window was a tiny gray kitten from Mary's house. I forgot all about prayer and said, "That's one of the kittens that I was playing with at Mary's." Daddy cleared his throat to get my attention, and spoke louder to finish our grace. Daddy ignored the kitten as it sat on our window and watched us eat our entire meal. I, on the other hand, kept leaning over George, staring, smiling, and occasionally, saying, "Hi, kitty." George suggested that he and I change places. We both looked at Mama and she nodded her head with approval. After dinner, I asked to be excused and ran outside to play with the kitten. Mama came out and told me I had better take it home before it got dark. I put the little gray kitten into the white basket tied to the front of my bike and took him home.

The very next night at dinner the little gray kitten joined us again. Pretty soon he became our regular guest at dinner time, sitting quietly on the ledge as we ate dinner, meowing once or twice, just to make sure that we knew he was there. Every night after dinner I took the kitten that Mary named "Grayish" back home. When he no longer fit into the basket, I carried him in my arms. One day I knocked on the door, "Here's your cat again," I laughed, jokingly. My friend's mother shook her head in disbelief, "I think this cat has chosen you to be his mom. Do you want to keep him?" I couldn't believe it. I was so excited that I ran back home to ask. Mama talked to Daddy and with a little convincing they both said, "Yes." Butch and I sat outside that night, playing with Grayish as we tried to think of a new name for him. Butch thought up the name "Tomcat" and so that's what we renamed him, "Tomcat." He became my best friend and he was the one that I talked to when Mama and Daddy would fight or when I felt lonely and scared.

20
Stabbed with the Screwdriver

When we lived in Bradenton, we went to the beaches on Anna Maria Island. On one side of the Island was Tampa Bay, and the other side was the Gulf of Mexico. Mama and Daddy liked a beach on Tampa Bay best, because it wasn't very crowded. There wasn't a lifeguard or beach patrol; therefore, they could drink beer without getting in trouble. There was a law against bringing alcoholic drinks onto the beach. We usually went to a beach we called Sandspur Beach. In order to get to the sand and water, you first had to cross a grassy area that was loaded with prickly sandspurs. Right down the road from Sandspur Beach was an old, grayish-brown, wooden pier. The pier held a bait shop and restaurant. We often would take a break from swimming and walk down to the pier and watch the brown pelicans that sat patiently waiting for handouts from fishermen. We often brought my cousins Eddie, Cindy and Tommie Lee to the beach with us. Eddie was the same age as Butch, Cindy was almost George's age and Tommie Lee was six weeks younger than me.

One day Eddie brought his fishing pole and bought a few shrimps at the small bait shop on the pier. He caught a pin fish, a small silver fish that's full of bones and about the size of a person's palm. After taking the fish off his hook, he put a small cut in the side of the pin fish with his knife. The blood dripped onto Eddie's hand and then down into the bluish gray water of Tampa Bay. Eddie then put the hook right underneath the dorsal fin of the pin fish and cast his line back out. He was using

69

the pin fish as bait in hopes of catching a much bigger fish. My brothers and I waited for Eddie to get a bite. His pole bent slightly from the pull of the pin fish swimming awkwardly away from the pier.

Soon the wooden planks beneath my bare feet grew much too hot to stand and wait. I would balance on my right foot, letting my left foot cool off, and then I'd switch feet. It wasn't long before I was begging my brothers to take me back down to the warm, soothing water. We were just off the pier and entering the water when we heard the commotion. We couldn't see who or what, but we knew that someone had caught something big. We ran out of the water and back onto the pier. There we saw Eddie grasping his pole that was bent so far over that it looked liked it was going to snap in two pieces! Wow! We were all excited. What is it, I wondered?! We ran over and butted in front of the crowd that was beginning to gather around him. That day Eddie brought up the biggest fish I had ever seen anyone catch; a four and a half foot shark!

The closest beach to us in Sanford was New Smyrna. Daddy had the day off so we decided to drive over to the beach. Mama and I made sandwiches for lunch. We packed some red plums, potato chips and generic cokes. We left early in the morning because Daddy didn't like to drive in traffic. Before we left Sanford we stopped at the Seven-Eleven® to get some candy bars for the trip and some beer for the cooler. Mama and Daddy decided to buy an extra six-pack for the car ride over to the beach.

Daddy's "almost new," white, medium-sized Ford looked like a box. He bought it from his company. Daddy's company, Mid Valley, would sell the old company cars to employees. Daddy said that this car was a "good deal." The interior was dark blue. The front seat was big enough to hold Daddy, Mama and me. Mama made me sit in the middle of the front seat because she said she was sick of hearing me fight with the boys when I sat between them in the back.

There were times that I liked sitting in the front seat. If Daddy was driving, we would have the air conditioner on and it was nice to have the cool air. Daddy was such a big man, and he just couldn't stand the heat, so when he drove the air conditioner was on. However, when he wasn't in the car he made it clear to Mama that the air conditioner wasn't needed. His thought was, he paid for the gas, he could use the air conditioner whenever he wanted. When we paid for the gas we could do the same. Another positive to sitting up front was that Mama let me control the radio stations. I loved finding the songs that I liked best and passing by the ones that the boys liked. There were also times that I didn't like sitting in the front seat. If Mama and Daddy were fighting, then it wasn't fun to sit in the front seat right in the line of fire.

Daddy was excited to get to the beach and try out his new toy. He had bought an old reel to reel movie camera from his brother, my Uncle Raymond, who lived in Tallahassee and owned an electronics store.

The ride over to New Smyrna was quiet. Mama sang along with the songs on the radio as I listened. Every now and then she'd stop to take a swig of beer or light up a cigarette. Butch stared out the back seat window on the driver side and George stared out the other window. They only spoke occasionally. Daddy drank his beer and drove.

Finally, we arrived at the beach. My brothers loved to swim at New Smyrna, but I didn't like it much. New Smyrna beach was on the Atlantic, which meant the east coast of Florida. The waves were much higher than at Sandspur Beach.

New Smyrna wasn't as murky as Sandspur but it was twice as rough and twice as dangerous. At New Smyrna, it wasn't sharks that we worried about, it was the undertow. The undertow would come unsuspectingly. It was as though some creature lived in the sand and when you were playing and not paying attention, it would come up and grab you. It would pull hard at the sandy floor, wrap its watery arms around your legs and pull you out deep and under the water. The undertow came in fast and caused a great current that made it difficult to swim to the shallow waters of safety.

Mama was lying out on the beach towel as the boys and I played in the water. Butch stood in the shallow waters and would toss me into the air just as a wave was coming in. Butch would throw me up backwards, I would throw my feet up and over my body, flipping in the air and then securely landing in the soft bed of the ocean wave. I could do this a hundred times, but he would tire of it much too soon. Then I would beg George to take his turn at playing with me.

One of the best aspects of the beach was the challenge of finding starfish and sand dollars. My technique was to shuffle my bare feet against the ocean floor and dig my toes into the sand. Occasionally, I would feel the hard body of a shell, or the spiny legs of the starfish or the round corners of the sand dollar. Sometimes, I even felt a crab. When that happened, the crab and I would both scuttle away as fast as we could! Once I discovered a treasure, I would either pick it up with my toes or dive underwater and pick it up. Once it was in hand, I would surface and holler for the entire family, "Look! Look!" After showing it off, I would dive back down and place it safely on the sandy floor bottom. If the starfish, sand dollar, or shell was really big, we would run it up to the shore so that Daddy could get a picture of it. After displaying our trophy, one of the boys would swim with it out past the sandbar and replace it on the ocean bottom so that it could continue to grow in peace and harmony.

After we played for some time, Mama called us in to eat lunch. After lunch, Mama always made us wait at least a half hour. She said that we would get stomach cramps and might drown if we went swimming right after we ate. That half hour always seemed to go the slowest! Often we would pass the time by burying each other up to our necks in the sand. Daddy was busy videotaping everything we did.

It wasn't long after lunch before Mama and Daddy began to fight about Daddy and the video camera. Mama said that Daddy was videotaping some women wearing bikinis and Daddy denied that he would ever do such a thing. (Later the film revealed that Daddy was indeed videotaping women in bikinis, but that was a different fight altogether.) As I sat there building a sand castle listening to them argue back and forth, I knew that it wouldn't be long before Mama would pack things up and want to go home. It was times like that, that I hated riding home in the front seat and dreaded the ride back to Sanford.

Mama hollered for me and the boys to start packing up the car. Slowly, we picked up our towels and started packing things away. The boys were quiet, and I could tell that they were mad. They wanted to stay and swim longer, but they couldn't say a word or they would get in the middle of the fight between Mama and Daddy. The last thing we wanted to do was to ride in the car for over an hour and listen to them fight. It was always the same thing: Daddy would sit behind the wheel looking straight ahead, trying not to have a reaction to Mama screaming at him and that day proved to be no different from any other.

Even though Daddy had the air conditioner on, the boys had their windows cracked. Both Mama and Daddy smoked. Butch and George said that the smoke irritated them, so they would crack their windows to get a little fresh air. Daddy would usually tell them to roll up the windows, but today, he didn't say a word. Mama was turned toward Daddy, complaining about him flirting with other women. She sat with her left knee up on the seat, giving me very little room to move. It was as though she couldn't see me or had forgotten I was there. She smoked a cigarette and took a couple swigs of the last beer. As Daddy ignored Mama, she began to complain louder, and louder, using more and more obscenities.

"You little peck--, son of a b---h!" Mama hollered out. Daddy sat there with no reaction. The quieter Daddy was, the madder Mama got. She accused him of sleeping with other women (she even named off my Aunt Marilyn) and then shouted out, "You'd sleep with every whore in town if you could!" Daddy still had no reaction. I heard a small sigh out of one of the boys in the back. He was probably thinking the same thing I was, "Mama is really pushing it." I could tell that Mama was trying to get a reaction out of Daddy. I sat there praying that Daddy would please give in and settle Mama down. "I tell you what Lorenzo, if I ever catch you fu-king around, I'll cut off your little p--ker!" She finally got a reaction out of Daddy. Without turning towards her, in a soft, yet irritated voice, Daddy said, "Shut up."

I really didn't understand what Mama was saying when she was yelling at Daddy. I knew that she was very mad and that she was using a lot of words that we weren't supposed to say. By then, every time Mama turned to say something to Daddy, I squeezed my eyes shut and tensed up every muscle in my body. I knew from experience that eventually she was going to hit something. In the past, it didn't matter if the car was moving or stopped. When Mama got mad, she would hit something or someone. With my eyes closed tight, I sat perfectly still, breathing slowly and trying not to move an inch. I knew that I couldn't cry, and I couldn't even hide my face in fear. I couldn't say a word or even let out a loud sigh.

Since Daddy was a big man, it took a lot to get him drunk. Mama on the other hand, had a very light tolerance. Mama continued on and Daddy had finally had enough of Mama's sharp tongue when he replied, "These kids don't need to hear you talkin' that way! Why don't you just save it for when we get home!" Mom laughed, "Home! You're not even gonna have a home, you co-- sucker! "Kids, did you know your father had sex with another man?" Daddy interrupted, "Carol, that's about enough! You're drunk!" Mama yelled, "When we get home, you're gonna pack your f---ing clothes and move the hell out!" Daddy replied back in an almost thankful attitude, "Fine, that's fine with me."

I sat stiffly with my hands to my side, my finger tips grasping onto seams that outlined each side of my seat. The muscles in my legs were at work keeping my feet flexed and still. Tears were streaming down my face. I didn't want Daddy to leave. I loved them both...Suddenly the car jolted to the right. The force of the swerve threw me into Daddy's side, and I opened my eyes thinking that we were in an accident. As Daddy slammed on the brakes, I saw a large, dirty, white brick wall just a foot in front of our car. Hand painted on the side of the building in big black letters were the words; ON/OFF SALE LIQUOR. It was a bar.

Mama asked, "What the hell are you doing?" As Daddy clumsily got out of the car, he told Mama that he was going into the bar to call the police. He wanted them to meet us at our house. He told Mama that she was crazy and for all he knew she would try to stab him again when we got home. At first, I felt relieved. I thought "Thank goodness! This will all be over soon." Then I realized that Daddy would be moving out, and I was torn between <u>wanting</u> the fight to stop and <u>not wanting</u> Daddy to leave.

I heard Butch say, after Daddy had shut the door and was out of ear's range, "This is bullsh--." Mama ignored Butch and sat in the car smoking her cigarette

75

while we waited for Daddy to come back. The car was starting to get hot and we couldn't turn on the air conditioner, because Daddy had taken the keys with him. He knew from experience that if he left the keys in the car, Mama would drive off and leave him there. We rolled down all the windows, and Mama had another cigarette.

Daddy was gone for a long time and Mama was steamin' mad. She didn't want to go into the bar because she didn't "look good enough to go in." Her shirt had gotten wet and sandy at the beach, so all she was wearing was her bikini top and shorts. She told the boys to go in and see what Daddy was doing in the bar. George went in to the bar and soon came back, "He's sittin' at the bar and said he would be out in just a minute." Mama called Daddy every name in the book as we waited and waited. Finally, she grabbed her purse off the floorboard, and pulled out her makeup bag. Brushing her matted hair and putting on lipstick, I knew she was preparing herself to go in and get Daddy out of the bar. Before leaving the car, Mama lit up a cigarette and went in. George exclaimed in a disappointed mutter, "Oh great, now we're going to be here all night."

It wasn't long before both Mama and Daddy were storming out of the bar. I let out a sigh of relief. I didn't feel like sitting in that hot car any longer, and I just wanted to go home. Daddy got in to drive home as Mama argued that he was too drunk to drive. I resumed my stiff and rigid position again as we continued to pull out of the bar and head for home. Mama yelled at Daddy for taking so long in the bar and Daddy kept repeating the same excuse over and over. "Someone was on the phone, so I sat down to have a couple of beers and wait for him to get off the phone." He also yelled at Mama for embarrassing him back there at the bar. Then Mama asked Daddy whom he was trying to impress. Mama asked if he found another woman back there that he wanted to sleep with? I closed my eyes. I didn't want to hear anymore. I was scared again.

Mama started to get another cigarette. She reached down into her purse, grabbed an empty pack and crumbled it up. She searched the bottom of her purse. She asked Daddy for one of his cigarettes and he said, "No." Throwing the empty pack at Daddy, she shouted, "You selfish son-of-a bit-h!" I watched Mama as she frantically searched the ash tray looking for a butt to smoke. I noticed Daddy roll down his window and I wondered what he was doing. With his window down, Daddy reached over to the ashtray, yanked it out and dumped it out his window. It was at that point I thought to myself, "Oh my God, there's gonna to be a war." I could feel my muscles tense up even more. Mama, frustrated and crying, opened the glove compartment throwing everything around. I thought she was looking for a cigarette; instead, she pulled out a screwdriver. The screwdriver was grasped tightly in her right hand, her eyes were thin and fierce. Without a word she moved fast, sliding over to the middle of the car, and squishing me into Daddy's side. She reached over me and crammed the screwdriver in Daddy's right nostril and yanked it out as hard as she could. With a great force, Mama flew back to her seat as her right arm hit the window. The screw driver made such a bang, I thought it was going to break the glass. Daddy screamed, grabbing his nose, "Oh my God, your crazy!" I felt something wet on my head and I reached up to feel it as I turned and looked at Daddy to see what was going on. Daddy was holding his nose and blood was dripping from his hand. Mama had just ripped open his right nostril with the screwdriver. Daddy slammed on the brakes and slid over to the side of the road just as George grabbed me by the shirt and began pulling me into the back seat. I took my hand off the wet spot on my head. It was covered with Daddy's blood. I frantically wiped it on the top of the front seat as George continued to pull me over.

Butch jumped out of the car, screaming that he had had enough. He started running away from the car when Daddy jumped out and ran after him. Mama rolled down the window and threw the screwdriver away. She sat there staring out the window, not looking at Butch running away or Daddy as he tried to run with his shirt up to his nose, trying to stop the bleeding.

Though I couldn't hear what Daddy said when he caught Butch, I could tell that their words weren't pleasant. Daddy grabbed Butch's arm and started to pull him back towards the car when Butch yanked his arm loose and walked back by himself. They both got back in the car and Butch slammed his door. Daddy looked over his shoulder but didn't say a word.

We were almost home when we passed a police officer. Upon seeing us he turned on his lights and quickly circled around behind us. Daddy pulled over. The policeman walked up to the car and asked if everything was all right. Daddy told him that Mama tried to kill him on the way home from the beach. The policeman followed Daddy home and sat inside talking to him and Mama for a long time. The boys and I sat outside on top of the hood of the car, waiting. The policeman finally came out and told us that everything was going to be just fine from now on. He said that our parents had talked and they promised they wouldn't fight anymore. Butch replied, "Yeah right!"

21
Accident on the Bridge

It was another one of those days that Mama promised to take us to the beach if we cleaned the house. The boys and I woke up early and began to clean as Mama slept in. I stood on a chair and washed the dishes as Butch stood beside me and dried. George worked hard on dusting and sweeping the floor. By the time Mama had woken up, we were finished with the house and had coffee made for her. Mama only found one thing to complain about and that was the hall closet. The big pile of clean clothes on the floor didn't get ironed and put away. Butch, thinking quickly, explained that we didn't want to wake her up by going in her room to get the ironing board. He told Mama that we planned on doing them after the beach. Mama accepted his answer and starting preparing sandwiches to take with us. Butch usually had a way of calming Mama down and talking his way out of a situation.

Right before we arrived at New Smyrna, Mama decided to make her usual stop at a bar for beer. She said it was early and that we had time for one or two. The boys and I were very disappointed but didn't say a word. There were many times that we did actually make it to the beach, but we never stopped being disappointed on those days that we had to stop at the bar. An hour had passed as Butch, George and I still sat in the car waiting. It was turning out to be another one of those days. Mama didn't like me to get out of the car, so I just sat in the car and either slept or daydreamed. Sometimes, I would imagine that I had different parents. I would imagine that my

79

parents were gone and I had to go live with my Aunt
Marilyn and cousins Eddie, Cindy and Tommie Lee.
Often, I wished I had parents like our church pastor and
his wife.

Hours later, Mama finally came stumbling out of
the bar. She was drunk. Butch and George were angry.
The day had come and gone. In order to go to the beach,
we had awakened early on a <u>Saturday</u> and cleaned the
entire house. Butch and George softly made a vow to
never fall for Mama's trick again.

Mama was so drunk she couldn't even drive
straight. The car swerving all over the road as she
attempted to drive home. We came to a small, narrow
bridge and the boys started yelling at Mama to watch out.
That bridge wasn't wide enough for two cars to pass at
the same time. I looked up just in time to see an oversized
truck on the bridge heading towards us. We were
crossing the bridge at the same time as a big truck. There
was no way we would make it!

I screamed as we sideswiped the truck and became
sandwiched between the truck and the side railing of the
bridge. Mama told Butch and George to get out of the car
and go find someplace to call Daddy. The boys ran across
the bridge to an old run-down house and there they
called Daddy to come and get us. I sat in the car as Mama
and the man argued over who was supposed to wait for
the other to pass.

22
Dangerous Fresh Water

We had to buy a new car. It wasn't exactly new, but it was nice. It was a brown four-door Buick. Being a one car family, Mama had to get up early to take Daddy to work. She wanted to make sure that he went straight to work and came straight home again.

We didn't go to the beach anymore on Saturdays. Instead, Mama found us a fresh water swimming hole to swim in. It was on the way to pick up Daddy, and usually, we were the only people there. You had to go down a narrow, bumpy road with ditches on each side to get to the swimming hole. The road was bumpy because it was made of shell and tar, and it hurt your feet when you got out of the car. The water at the swimming hole was nothing like the beach. This water was brown instead of greenish blue. Instead of being clear, it was cloudy and murky. The boys made a rope swing from a tree. I used to swing from the rope and even swim out way over my head, until one day I was frightened half to death.

Mama always sat in the car or on the shore as the boys and I swam. We would swim for an hour or two before leaving to go pick up Daddy. One hot day we talked Mama into stopping at the swimming hole for a little while. We didn't have our bathing suits, so we swam in our shorts. The boys were climbing the tree to jump into the water. Mama was sitting on the sand watching me as I swam. I walked out until I was in about neck deep of water as I heard Butch and George screaming, "Snake! Looks like a Moccasin!" My back was to the shore, so I turned around facing the bank as Mama jumped up shouting, "Where?" We all knew what a Water Moccasin was. It was one of the most dangerous snakes in Florida. Mama had told us about articles in the newspaper about swimmers being bitten by them when they were splashing around in the water. Knowing that the snake was in the water, I didn't move. I didn't want to swim right into it. I glanced to the right, then left, then I heard the boys shout, "It's right by Cheri!" Mama yelled out, "CHERI!" That's when I saw it. It was less than two feet away from me in the murky brown water. It was long and black and it glided across the top of the water. It blended so well, it was difficult to keep an eye on. If it weren't for it's movement, I wouldn't have seen it at all. It swam in the form of an S. I stood still, holding my breath, hoping that it wouldn't notice me. Mama and the boys were quiet, and I think they were holding their breath, too. It was within a foot of my shoulder as its body smoothly and gracefully swam by me. It swam in front of me and over to an area where a tree had fallen. Mama ran out and grabbed me out of the water.

23
Stupie

We went back to the swimming hole a couple times, but I never went into the water again. Instead, I would walk along the road and ditch and look for shells and interesting things. One day I found something wonderful! As I walked along the road looking for small treasures, I heard a slight meow off to my right in the mangrove. I ran back to the beach and got Mama. I told her that I thought I heard a meow. Our swimming hole was out in the middle of nowhere, so there couldn't have been any tame cats out there. When Mama and I went over to check it out, we heard a faint, "meow." We couldn't see anything, but we could hear what sounded like a small kitten. Mama said that someone must have come out and dumped off kittens, so she called the boys over to help us look for them. We crossed the ditch, and that's when a kitten came stumbling out of the mangrove; a gray and white tabby kitten. It couldn't have been over ten weeks old. It was tiny and very thin. Mama said that it would probably die, but that we could take it home and try to nurse it back to health. We left the swimming hole, went to a store and got it some milk. The kitten couldn't drink it out of a bowl, so Mama showed me how to dip my finger into the milk and let the kitten lick it off my finger.

Needless to say, Daddy wasn't thrilled to find out we had another cat. I told Daddy that, if he let me keep it, that I would let him name it. That's how my cat got the name "Stupid," but I called him Stupie, for short.

Light Beyond the Darkness

24
The Day I Made Friends with Jesus

It was one of the last few times that my family attended church *together.* I was almost eight years old and it was the day that I decided to walk up the aisle during the Benediction. Each Sunday, at the end of the service, our preacher asked people to come up to the altar during the Benediction. There he would kneel and pray with those who came forward. Each person would ask for forgiveness for their sins, and, believing that Jesus died for those sins, they would ask Him to come into their heart. By asking Jesus into their heart, they were starting over in a new life as a born- again Christian.

As I stood there in church with my head bowed, my eyes closed, and my hands clasped together, the congregation was singing "Just As I Am." Our preacher stood up at the altar praying for the congregation, and I silently said my prayer to God. "Please, dear Lord, help my Mama and Daddy not to fight, please help my brothers to get along, and please, please let us be a normal family." I started to cry and I didn't even know why. As the tears trickled down my cheeks, I felt something wonderful come over me. It was a calm and relaxing sensation that filled me with warmth, hope and peace. Something inside me wanted to go up and accept Jesus Christ into my heart. Standing next to the aisle that led to the altar, I was scared to make that first step. A silent alarm went off in my head warning me that, if I went up the aisle, my parents would be mad and my brothers would be embarrassed. Yet, that sweet serene feeling in my heart urged me to go. I hesitated only for a

moment before I stepped out into the aisle, and, with my
head bowed to the floor, I started walking forward to the
altar to be saved. Half way up the aisle, fearful that my
parents would be mad, I turned back to look at Mama.
Instead of being angry, I saw tears as they swelled in her
eyes and she nodded to me in approval. I went up to the
altar and the preacher asked me if I believed what it said
in Romans 10:9-10. He proceeded to tell me the verse and
we prayed aloud and that's the day I made friends with
Jesus.

> *Romans 10:9-10 (NIV)*
> *That if you confess with your mouth, "Jesus*
> *is Lord," and believe with your heart*
> *that God raised Him from the dead, you*
> *will be saved.*
> *I John 5:11 (KJV)*
> *And this is for the record. God has given*
> *us eternal life, and this life is in His*
> *Son. He who has the Son has eternal*
> *life. He who does not have the son,*
> *does not have eternal life.*

Weeks later, at my baptism, my family attended
church together for one of the very last times. Mama said
that she and Daddy didn't go to church anymore because
people in our congregation made fun of us for attending a
tent revival. The reason we went to the tent revival was
because Daddy was sick and Mama had heard that they
would have healing there. Daddy's legs were turning
black and blue. The doctor said that it was due to poor
circulation and to the fact that Daddy had very thick
blood. Daddy had to wrap his legs in ace bandages every
single day. Daddy wouldn't even wear shorts anymore.
Mama said that the doctor also told Daddy that he
probably wouldn't live to the age of forty but I didn't
know why.

At the revival Daddy wouldn't go up to the altar when the preacher called for those individuals that needed healing. Mama sat there urging him and so did I, but he wouldn't go. On the other hand, I begged Mama to let me go, "Isn't there anything that I need to be healed for?" I asked as I nudged her on the leg. Mama just answered softly, "No, Cheri, you're gonna be just fine."

Though Mama and Daddy didn't attend church, Mama said that it was important for us kids to go and learn about God. Our church had a bus, and it came right to our house to pick us up. I didn't mind going to church without our parents; I liked church, but, the boys didn't like to go at all. They thought Mama was just being a hypocrite. Some Sundays the boys would complain their way out of going and on those days I would go by myself.

Light Beyond the Darkness

25
What a Horrible Birthday   March 1973

It was my eighth birthday. I got up early and put on a fancy blue dress to wear to church. Blue was my favorite color. Everyone in my family was still in bed. The boys were allowed to sleep late this Sunday, so that meant I was going to church by myself. Daddy had gone out drinking the night before and didn't get home till late. Once he got home, he and Mama fought for hours.

Bright and early I woke up, excited to celebrate my eighth birthday. I tried to wake up Mama so that she could make me breakfast but she said she would get up in a minute and then she never did. I figured she was too tired from all the arguing the night before so I went out into the kitchen and fixed a bowl of cereal for breakfast and sat on the couch to watch cartoons. Since I had gotten up so early, I had plenty of time. After breakfast, I decided to go out and feed the cats and play for a little while.

Tomcat was waiting outside the door for me. He was the most faithful cat. He followed me everywhere and would come running when I called out his name. I took his faithfulness for granted and paid more attention to Stupie. Stupie was my favorite cat. Sometimes he came when I called, and sometimes he didn't. He didn't really show any love or devotion to me but I knew he only liked two people in my family; Daddy and me. We were the only two people he would come to at all. Every time Stupie heard Daddy's voice, he would come running over and rub up against his legs. Daddy said it really irritated him but I think he felt special just like I did knowing that we were the only two people that Stupie would even get close to.

I poured cat food into the dish under the carport and called out for Stupie to come and eat; Tomcat was already eating. When Stupie didn't come, I started looking around for him. I laughed when I saw him lying in the grass near the side of the road. "You lazy cat," I said softly. I walked over and told Stupie to get up. He just lay there with his mouth open and his eyes half closed. "Stupie, what's wrong with you? Get up." Thinking that Stupie was too tired to get up, I nudged him with my shoe and said, "Get up Stupie." His body was stiff. I still didn't realize what was wrong until I bent down beside him; I saw ants. "STUPIE!" I cried as I ran into the house. I ran all the way back to my parents' room, pushed open the door, and rushed to their bed. "Stupie's dead! Stupie's dead!" Mama was groggy and Daddy didn't move at all. I shook Mama, "Did you hear me? Someone killed Stupie!" With his eyes still closed, Daddy turned to me and said, "Good." Mama rolled over and nudged Daddy hard. "Lo!"

Then it dawned on me that Daddy was out drinking all night. I sat there for just a moment crying and thinking... Daddy must have run over Stupie when he got home. I screamed at Daddy, "You killed him! You ran over him, didn't you?!" Mama tried to tell me it wasn't Daddy, but that someone else must have run over Stupie. "Don't worry Cheri, everything will be all right." I ran out of the room just as the church bus pulled up and honked its horn. I ran out of the house, not looking in the direction of Stupie, jumped on the bus and cried all the way to church. It was as though everyone had forgotten my birthday. I felt like no one cared and worst of all, my favorite cat had just died. What a horrible birthday!

26
Choo-Choo

Mama saw an ad in the paper for Pekinese puppies. Mama had always wanted a Pekinese. She talked Daddy into going to look at them. The puppies were in a cage under this lady's carport. Somehow, Daddy said that Mama could get one. Mama named her Choo-Choo (after the noise that a train makes). That dog loved Mama more than anything. As it grew older it began to protect Mama and all of Mama's belongings. It was the most loyal dog I had ever seen. However, Choo-Choo was a peculiar dog. She loved Mama and hated everyone else. If anyone ever came into the house, or near Mama, our little Choo-Choo would attack. Once my friend Mary came over, and instead of knocking on the door, she just walked in. "Cheri" she called out. Choo-Choo was the first to respond to my friend's call. I heard her little feet scratch against the hall floor as she tore into the living room. Choo-Choo stood guard growling at Mary until I walked out of the bathroom and yelled at Choo-Choo to stop growling. However, Choo-Choo wouldn't stop. Mary turned around and ran out the screen door. Choo-Choo was right on her heels and chased her around our house and up the tree in our back yard.

Choo-Choo was the only dog that I knew that snored louder than Daddy. It was irritating to everyone but Mama; she thought it was cute. Choo-Choo was also the only guard dog that I knew that protected its owner's purse. One day, Mama asked me to grab her purse and bring it into the kitchen for her. I walked over to Daddy's

Lazy Boy chair. Mama's purse lay on the floor next to it. No one was in the living room, or at least, that's what I thought. When my hand touched that purse, Choo-Choo, who was hiding behind the chair, watching for unsuspecting victims, charged at me. Viciously, she grabbed my forehead and I felt her teeth break into my skin. Screaming, I called for Mama to help me.

Sometimes, us kids felt as though Mama loved that dog more than she loved us. Daddy eventually had enough of the dog, "pooping and peeing on the floor" and made Mama give it away. It was obvious how upset Mama was, and when the day came for Choo-Choo to go to her new home, the boys asked permission to spend the night at their friend's house. They knew that something bad would happen when Mama had to give up her dog.

Knowing that Mama was both sad and mad at Daddy, I watched my Ps and Qs and tried to do everything correctly. Early in the morning, Mama and I left to drop Choo-Choo off. Mama cried all the way there, and then, on the way home she stopped and bought a six pack of beer. I knew that the beer would do one of two things; either it would make her forget Choo-Choo, or it would make Mama even more depressed. Unfortunately, it caused her to get more mad at Daddy and more depressed. The more depressed she became, the more she took her anger out on me.

As the morning grew later, and Mama drank more, I started counting the hours until Daddy would come home. I never felt safe alone in the house with Mama when she was drinking and depressed. All day I didn't ask to go anywhere. Without her having to tell me anything twice, I did everything Mama asked right away. I was trying to be on my best behavior. I folded and ironed all the clothes that had piled up in our laundry closet. I washed the dishes, swept the floor and made the beds. Mama spent most of the day in her room. Early in the afternoon, Mama ran out of beer so we went to a small, local bar. We didn't know anyone there because she hadn't been going out as much. However, it wasn't long before Mama met a man. He took her mind off Daddy and/or Choo-Choo and hopefully diverted her anger from me.

Hours passed. Daddy had gotten a ride to work with some other men so that Mama could use the car. It was almost 5:00 p.m. and I knew that was about the time he got off work. I was anxious to leave the bar and go home to Daddy. We left the bar and on the way home, Mama stopped to pick up dinner. Once home, we pulled in the driveway and parked under the carport.

I ran into the house as Mama hollered at me to come back and help with the food. I knew right away that Daddy wasn't home. When Mama found out that Daddy wasn't home, she threw the bag of fast food dinners all over the living room floor. I picked it up in silence and made each of us a plate for dinner. We waited and waited and, as we waited, things grew worse. Mama finally decided to leave. She said she was running up to the store for beer, and that I could stay home. She gave me strict instructions not to open the door for anyone. I didn't want to stay home alone, and I didn't want to go with Mama either. I felt so confused and scared. I sat on the couch watching television and I prayed for God to keep me safe. I dozed off on the couch. When I looked at the clock I realized that time had slipped by quickly. What seemed like a short nap was actually a few hours. It was dark outside.

As Mama walked in the house, she reeked of alcohol and smoke. She asked where Daddy was, and I said, "I don't know." Now Mama was really mad. She reached down grabbed my arm and yanked me off the couch. "Why aren't you in bed?" she growled as she dragged me back to my bedroom. She stumbled as she threw me onto the bed. She was mad at Daddy and taking it out on me. I stuffed my face into my pillow.

Mama fell onto my bed. She rolled onto her back and sounded as if she had just run a marathon and was completely out of breath. "I'm just going to lay here for a few minutes," she muttered as she seemed to drift off to sleep. Even with my face buried in my pillow, I could smell the aroma of the bar that we had visited earlier. My right side was squished against the wall. My arms were tucked tightly by my sides, and my hands were pressed together near my mouth. Softly, I said my prayer;

> *"Now I lay me down to sleep, I pray to the Lord my soul to keep.*
> *If I die before I wake, I pray the Lord my soul to take.*
> *Bless Mama, Bless Daddy, Bless Butchie, Bless Georgie, Bless Tomcat, Bless Stupie, Bless Choo-Choo, (I still asked God to bless them even though they were gone) Bless Blackie, (My new stray cat) Bless me...Amen."*

"What the hell are you doing?" Mama turned over and slapped me on the back of my head. "I'm praying." I cried without exposing my face. Mama asked accusingly, "Who are you praying to... the devil? Turn your -ss over!" She hit me in my back as she hollered at me for facing down while I prayed. "God is up in Heaven, not in Hell, Cheri. What are you, stupid?" She kept hitting me with her fist as I rolled over to my side. "Turn over!" She commanded. Curled up, almost into a ball, with my hands blocking my face, she hit me until I turned and laid flat on my back. I spoke, in a soft, painful voice, "Mama, you're hurting me, Mama, ouch." Then with one, final blow to my stomach she said, "Now start over and say them right!" I couldn't breathe, the last hit took me by surprise and knocked the wind right out of me. Mama repeated, "Say your prayers!" When I didn't say a word, she turned, looked at me, and quickly sat me up and began slapping me on my back. I took in a long deep breath and I felt my entire body aching with pain. Mama didn't make me say my prayers again. She said she would go get me a glass of water but she never came back into my room.

27
Sounds Like a Fresh Start

Daddy received a promotion. Everyone was happy until he told us that we would be moving again. Butch and George were disappointed because they had met some good friends and hated to start over. Daddy argued that the high school in Sanford had too much crime and violence. Not long ago, Butch saw a boy stab one of his teachers in the stomach with a hunting knife. There were a lot of racial fights at the high school, too.

I don't think Mama wanted to leave Sanford either. She had begun her own identity and that was important to her. She had passed her GED test, had gone on to nursing school, and passed with flying colors. She graduated and went on to work part-time in the evening as an LPN. I was the only one who supported Daddy and wanted to move. I felt sorry for Daddy. It seemed that no one was ever on his side. He couldn't help it if we had to move. Besides, things weren't going well for me in Sanford. The kids at school didn't like me. Many of them played tricks on me and called me names. I suppose the kids didn't like the way I looked. I usually dressed myself in the morning. My hair was usually pretty tangled and since it was us kids job to iron the clothes, my outfits were usually wrinkled. However, there were days that Mama would get up and help me get ready for school. She would lay out freshly ironed clothes (that she got up and ironed) and brush my hair. My long tangled hair usually frustrated Mama so much that she'd just wind up hitting me in the head with the hair brush.

Some mornings Mama was up early and baking or cooking breakfast, other mornings she had what she called, "The Flu." Basically, it was a hangover. When

Mama had a hangover it meant two things to the boys and me. First, we had to call her in sick to work, and lie about her illness. Second, we would have to walk on egg shells all afternoon hoping not to upset her. Even though Mama was very unpredictable, there were some things we could predict very well.

Moving from Sanford sounded like a fresh start. Every time we moved, our family seemed to start out on the right foot. Maybe Mama and Daddy would start going to church again. Moving gave me hope.

28
Our New House in Palma Sola, Florida

Palma Sola, in Northwest Bradenton. It was like a dream come true. We finally had a new house, new school, new friends and a new life. Little did I know what was ahead.

Daddy and Mama met with a builder and decided on the layout of our house. It was in a new development in Palma Sola and there weren't very many houses in the area. Our only next door neighbors had two older boys and a younger girl. Her name was Theresa, and she was a couple years younger than me. There was an elderly couple across the street that were very nice and loved to have me come over and visit. There was an empty lot next to the elderly couple. After that was a house with an older daughter named Wendy. I visited her on occasion. Behind our house there was a family with a boy and two girls. They were from Michigan. They seemed to be a close family. The only other family was diagonally behind us. They were an older couple with no children living at home. The rest of the neighborhood consisted of empty lots that grew high with sawgrass and weeds.

I was so excited when the day came that we could finally move in. We pulled into our newly paved driveway, which curved like a half of a horseshoe and stopped in front of our garage. Our first garage! The house was white stucco brick with shining paint that sparkled when the sun beat down upon it. From the front you could see deep, rusty colored shutters that were the same color as our heavy, wooden, front and garage door. Our first garage! They all matched beautifully with the red brick that outlined our entry way and front room window. "Wow!" I thought to myself, "This can't be our house!"

Daddy wouldn't let us go in until he told us how he was going to landscape the front yard and entry way garden. We all dreamed with Daddy as we walked around the house and he named off the ferns and palms that he wanted to plant. He wanted us to imagine the smell of orange blossoms as our future tangelo tree grew to shade a portion of our back yard. Our anticipation grew heavier and heavier. We really wanted to go into the house and take a look around. It wasn't long before I was begging Daddy to let us go inside. Daddy made us run around to the front where we had to close our eyes until he unlocked the door, guided each of us in and exclaimed in a proud, fatherly voice, "Tah Dah!" I opened my eyes and beamed as I looked around.

We stepped inside onto the deep, blue, shag carpet. To our left was our living room and to our right was the dining room. We walked into the dining room. It was roomy and on one wall was a built-in pantry with sliding doors. There were two doors in our dining room; one led to the garage, and the other led to my parents' room. Adjacent to the dining room was our modern looking kitchen. Daddy explained to us how the drop-ceiling lights were the newest thing. But, best of all, we had a built-in dishwasher!

Next, we ventured into our parents' room. It was a big bedroom. They had a large walk-in closet and another closet to keep their bathroom accessories in. Their adjacent bathroom was small but efficient. I thought it was strange that they only had a shower and no tub. Mama and Daddy decorated their room with Mama's favorite color. They had long, red, shag carpet and heavy, red drapes that covered both the windows in their room. Mama was planning to buy a red bedspread to match.

We walked out of our parents' room, through the dining room, through the living room, turned right into a spacious brown, paneled room that we called the Florida room. Some people called this our family room. Mama said we'd keep our television and furniture in that room. The Florida room had big windows that opened up to our bare, back yard. All the windows in the house were new. I told Daddy how much I loved that I didn't have to crank the windows opened now. Instead, all I had to do to open them was slide them up. Daddy told me that I would be happy to know that this house had central heat and air. I didn't know what he meant, but the boys were surely excited about it. Off the Florida room, there was a door that led to our back yard.

Now we were going to look at the best part of the house, my room. We left the Florida room and entered our small hall. To the right was a bathroom. It had yellow carpet and a yellow countertop. It was bright, and had both a shower and a bathtub. I couldn't believe we had such a modern looking bathroom. Next was my room. I was thrilled to see my blue walls and blue shag carpet. Though it wasn't an ordinarily large room, it was the biggest room I had ever lived in. My closet had two doors that slid open from the center, and I had two windows. I loved my room from the first day I saw it. The final room was the boys' room. It was a little larger than my room. They had two windows also. One of their windows faced the driveway, and the other faced the field next door. They had white walls and blue carpet.

It wasn't long before we were shopping with green stamps. Mama had saved a lot of green stamps, so we went to the store and bought a few new things for the house, a new bedspread for me, and a basketball for the boys. We also shopped at discount stores for items to put in the house. Mama decided to decorate the living room with a Spanish accent.

29
Misleading Games

At first, It felt good to be back in Bradenton. I had a lot of family in Bradenton that I liked to spend time with. Aunt Marilyn was my mom's sister. She believed in God and always told me that she would pray for me. She was afraid of Mama. As young girls growing up, Aunt Marilyn had witnessed a hateful side of Mama. Over the years she shared with me some of the terrible memories that she had from childhood, such as: Mama pushing her into an alligator pond for singing at the wrong time and beating up five boys with a stick. She also shared about the terrible relationship between Mama and Pop-Pop. I was told that Pop-Pop would beat Mama something terrible. Because of the past and the fact that Aunt Marilyn's daughters Cindy and Tommie Lee were frightened of Mama too, I usually spent the night at their house instead of them coming over to our house.

While I had lived in Sanford, Aunt Marilyn had divorced my Uncle Jerry and married "Bob" (he lived across the field from Aunt Marilyn's house with his wife and kids and he too had divorced his first wife). At first, I really liked Aunt Marilyn's new husband. He was nice and seemed to pay a lot of attention to Cindy, Tommie Lee and I. However, it wasn't long before I felt uncomfortable around Uncle Bob. It was hard to put my finger on just why I felt so uncomfortable around him. Was it the way he looked at me? Was it because he walked around in his underwear (Uncle Bob worked nights)? Perhaps it was in the way he reached out to touch me in my private areas when I passed him in the hall? I could tell that Tommie

Lee was confused by Uncle Bob's actions, too. She was afraid to be alone with him. When it came time for Uncle Bob to drive me home, Tommie Lee and I would argue about who was going to have to sit up front next to Uncle Bob. Neither one of us wanted to sit in the front seat of the car with him. We both knew he would reach over and touch us, but we never talked about it. Sometimes, Tommie Lee would make up an excuse why she couldn't go with Uncle Bob to take me home, and then I would have to ride home alone with him. I would beg Tommie Lee to go with us but she didn't want to ride back alone with him. Often I would ask Aunt Marilyn to take me home but she had problems of her own (Aunt Marilyn would sit in closets and not talk to anyone for hours). So, Uncle Bob would drive me home and, as I sat there staring out the window he would small talk with me. The drive would take fifteen to twenty minutes. Then Uncle Bob would always start the game. It began with tickling. He would reach over and try to squeeze his fingers under my biceps and into my armpit. "Are you ticklish?" He would ask with a smile. I would squirm away from Uncle Bob, getting closer to the window, trying desperately to get out of his reach. I'd say "No, I'm not really ticklish." Then he would move on to another game. He would bypass my arm altogether and reach over and touch other areas. "Are you ticklish there? Most girls like to be tickled there." I hated when he touched me. What was I supposed to do? I can remember thinking, "Does every girl get tickled? Am I weird?" I was so confused.

Many years later, Tommie Lee opened up and told her mom about the touching and misconduct of Uncle Bob. Aunt Marilyn believed her and confronted my Uncle. Through love, sacrifice and the grace of God, this family experience forgiveness and healing. I am so proud of my Uncle and my Aunt for not giving up on their marriage, for not turning their back on the family unit. There was a serious problem and we all suffered from that problem. Yet, through forgiveness, we can all be healed. We can love and most importantly trust again.

Light Beyond the Darkness

30
Nod My Head and Smile

Daddy's promotion was supposed to mean that everything was going to get better, yet things just kept getting worse. I felt alone like never before. Daddy was gone all the time. Many days he would work overtime. Daddy continued to stop at the bar after work and stay there late, regardless of the consequences at home. Then Daddy started a second job as a tree excavator. Every weekend Daddy would work at his second job that he called, "Tree Surgery." He worked and worked and worked.

Butch and George were going to Manatee High School. After school, Butch worked as a bag boy at Wynn Dixie® on Manatee Ave. He saved up enough money to buy himself a car. That allowed him and George to be away from home most of the time. I was in third grade at Palma Sola Elementary. It seemed like I never saw anyone except Mama. She worked as a nurse at the local hospital. However, Mama didn't work at any one place too long. She always found something that she didn't like and she would quit. As a result she worked all over Bradenton and Sarasota. She worked at the hospitals, nursing homes, and she even tried private duty nursing. The boys said that Mama couldn't keep a job because she drank too much. Regardless of her drinking, everywhere Mama worked she seemed to be well liked and regarded as a good nurse.

During the weeks that Mama was out of work, I would often come home from school and find Mama in her housecoat with messy hair and yesterday's smeared-on makeup. There she sat at the table with an ashtray full of butts in front of her. Often she would wait till I got home from school to get dressed. Then she would take me to the bars to "hang out." We would either go to Ray's Bar and Grille, Josie's, or Stella's. They were <u>all</u> in the worst parts of town and looked like they should have a "condemned" sign on the outside. For some reason, I didn't mind going to Ray's. As I walked in, I saw the same faces; staring, laughing, even sitting in the same places. I wondered how they could stay the same when I had gone through so many moves, and so many changes. Part of me felt sorry for those people. It was as though they were washing their dreams and their hopes away with one more glass of beer. Though I could see loneliness and depression in their eyes, they had loving and friendly hearts. Little did I know, that just as they used alcohol to escape their world, I used them to escape my own.

Tommie Lee hated going to the bars with us. She hated the strangers, dirty floors and drunk people. I'd get mad at Tommie Lee for not wanting to go with us. I wanted someone my age to go to the bars with us. Though I liked the people, it was still pretty boring. Besides, Tommie Lee asked me to do things for her all the time <u>and I did</u>. She never wanted to spend the night at my house, so I always stayed at her house. She was afraid to ask Uncle Bob for stuff, so I always asked for her. When she asked me to call the boys she liked, I even did that for her. I felt angry that she would not go to the bars with Mama and me.

Looking back, I can understand why Tommie Lee was frightened to frequent Ray's with us. Most of the time the people were so drunk, we couldn't even understand them and besides, there wasn't really anything to do. It was a low income area and it was scary. Many of the people just got off work or had poor hygiene and their body odor was difficult to take, yet I learned a great lesson from them. I learned the best thing to do was to just nod my head and smile. They always smiled back and their lonely life seemed better, even if it was just for a moment. I learned to be friendly to others, and not to judge them by their appearance. To me, Ray's Bar and Grille was a safe place. While at the bar, Mama was usually sweet. She never raised her voice at me and often gave me quarters to go play games and the jukebox.

The only one unpredictable thing about Ray's; you never knew who Mama would bring home. Mama felt sorry for a lot of the old men and would bring them home to eat dinner or have a beer. I'll never forget "Peck." He had a knot on his forehead and I think that's why people called him, "Peck." He was always drunk and never once could I understand what he had to say. He was much older and liked to play our piano. If Daddy or anyone said something negative about Peck, Mama would defend him by explaining that he had a good heart.

You could never tell what would happen after a day at Ray's. If Mama stayed too late at the bar, she knew that Daddy would be mad. To avoid Daddy, Mama and I would spend the night at someone else's house. Most of the time, we would spend the night at Grandma California's house. Mama would tap on Grandma's window to wake her up and Grandma would make a pallet on the floor for us. Other times, it wasn't so good. Mama would meet a man and we would sleep at his house. I would sleep on his couch.

I never told my friends in the neighborhood that we went to the old, falling down bars on the east side of town, yet, I rarely complained to Mama about having to go with her. Now that everyone in my family was gone most of the time, it was almost a relief for Mama and I to go to the bar. If she didn't drink at the bar, she would drink at home. When Mama was lonely, she took her problems out on me.

Light Beyond the Darkness

31
Don't Speak Louder than a Whisper

Since Daddy and the boys left early for work and school, it was my job to wake up Mama every morning. I was supposed to go in and wake her up precisely at 7:50a.m. Waking Mama up wasn't a pleasant job. She was unpredictable. Sometimes she would be as pleasant as a lamb, and other days she would be as raging as a Tasmanian devil. On those days, she could always find something to get angry about; either I would wake her up too early, too late, or I was too slow at getting dressed. It was my responsibility to feed the cats and my gerbil in the morning. Often I would forget to feed them before I woke up Mama; that too infuriated Mama. Other times, I forgot to make her a fresh pot of coffee. It seemed as though I couldn't do anything right.

One October evening, Daddy returned from a business trip to Pensacola. He brought me a beautiful, blue and white, pin-striped, sailor dress. I was delighted when I saw it. Daddy had never bought something for me without me first having to ask for it. I thought that it was a sign that he really loved me. Daddy brought something back for Mama too, but Mama didn't like it. She thought that he had slept with another woman and was trying to make up for it. Mama and Daddy began to fight about the presents and during their fight, I made a plan to make Mama feel better. I decided that I would get up early the next morning and make sure that everything was perfect when she woke up. I thought if I could just do everything right for once, then she would be happy.

The next morning Daddy came into my room, pretending to play the bugle. In his off-tune, gentle voice, he tooted as if playing the bugle, "It's time to get up, it's time to get up, it's time to get up in the morning." He flipped the light switch on and off and began the verse again. I remained in bed until I remembered my plans and my new dress that I was going to wear to school. Then, anxiously, I leapt out of bed and said, "Good morning!"

Daddy said he would make me a bowl of cereal while I fed my gerbil. After he and the boys left, I tiptoed into the kitchen and made a fresh pot of coffee for Mama. She and Daddy each could drink a whole pot of coffee in the morning. Mama liked hers strong, and Daddy liked his a little weaker. I quietly opened the door off the dining room to go out to the garage. There I fed Tomcat and then quietly went back into the house to put on my new dress. First, I found a pair of white socks in my top drawer. They weren't lacy as I would have liked, but they matched the dress. I dug my dress shoes out of my closet and put on the new sailor dress. I went into the bathroom and brushed my teeth and my hair.

There. Everything was ready and I had five minutes before it was time to wake up Mama. I walked into the Florida room and even before turning on the television, I turned the volume knob down low. It was a trick that Butch and George had taught a long time ago. Quietly, I sat a foot away from the television on a pillow. The volume of the television was so low I could hardly hear it. There was a clock on the wall above the television. I looked up at the clock. It was almost ten till eight. I had about two minutes left. I watched a cartoon until a commercial came on, then I remembered about Mama. It was 7:55 a.m. I jumped up, flipped off the television and ran into her room. "Mama, time to wake up," I said in a soft but rushed voice. I was hoping that Mama wouldn't get mad at me today because I had already gotten dressed, fed the cats and the gerbil, and made the coffee. She didn't have to comb my hair or anything. I had done everything, and so she got to sleep an extra five minutes!

Mama looked up at me from her bed. Her eyes went from my head to my new dress. Quickly, she rolled over and looked up at the digital clock that was up on Daddy's dresser. "You woke me up late, again." She said in a disgusted voice. "Can't you do anything right?" She asked. "You're just like your..." I interrupted, thinking to myself, she must not have noticed that I'm already dressed and ready for school. "Mama, I made your coffee, and got dressed. I fed the animals and even brushed my hair. Daddy made my breakf.." She interrupted as she threw the covers off, putting her legs on the floor, and sat up in bed, "You can't do anything right." Tears welled up in my eyes as I tried to explain to her. "But Mama, I.." Then, SLAP! Mama 's hand hit my face. "Don't talk back to me, Little Girl!" She yelled out, emphasizing the words, <u>Little Girl</u>. "Yes." I replied as tears streamed down my flushed cheeks. The blow to my face hurt, but not as much as my feelings. It was hard to control my crying. It always made Mama madder when I cried hard or hyperventilated. So I stood there, mouth closed, breathing. Mama stood above me, "Yes? Yes what?! Don't just say 'yes' to me!" "Yes, Mama, I mean, yes Ma'am?" I whispered, wondering which answer she really wanted. I stood bent over not knowing what was going to come next.

"Are you trying to make fun of me? You don't respect me, do you? I can tell you don't respect me." "Mama, I'm not trying to make fun of you." I answered softly, in a defenseless voice. "The only person you respect is your FATHER, and he doesn't even love you! Did you hear me?" I didn't answer because I didn't know what to say. It wasn't true, but Mama would be mad if I defended Daddy, so, with tears still falling, I looked down at the floor and put my hands up to my face.

"That dress looks terrible on you!" Mama was starting to yell now. She wanted to get an answer out of me, but I didn't know what to say. "He doesn't even know what size dress you wear!" Pause. "He doesn't really love you!" Pause. Now yanking down on my dress, Mama laughed and mockingly said to me, "It's way too small for you, you know that, don't you? Or maybe you want boys to look at you. Is that it, Cheri?"

Oh, I felt so bad. Why was Mama saying those things to me? Doesn't she know she's hurting my feelings? My heart pounded and with every thump, it became more difficult for me to hold in the sobs of anger. For whatever reason, Daddy thought of me and bought me a dress and I loved it. Then suddenly, I couldn't hold it back any longer. I threw my hands down frantically trying to push Mama's hands off my dress. At the same time, I finally let out cries of anguish.

That's when Mama came after me. First, came her fists, hitting my shoulders, then my ribs, screaming at me as she swung, "Cry little baby! Cry! Cry... for your father who doesn't even love you! The only person that he loves is himself!"

I hid my face again with my hands, and I begged Mama to stop, "Please Mama, please don't...I'm sorry!" Hysterically, I tried to tell her that I only wanted to make her happy. I tried to do everything for her. Mama grabbed me by the hair and yanked me out of the corner. She held my hair up high over my head. It was so painful that I thought my hair was going to come right out of my scalp. "Owww, Please Mama!"

She pulled me over to the opposite side of the room where a large pile of clean clothes lay in the corner on the floor. It was a pile of clothes that needed to be ironed and hung up. "If you wanted to help, why didn't you iron these damn clothes? You little brat," she yelled out as she let go of my hair and pushed me into the clean clothes. "I'm sorry Mama, I'm sorry. I'll do them after school." I whimpered, pleading with her not to hurt me anymore. Mama turned around with her back to me. She bent over from her waist and picked up one of Daddy's size 16 shoes. Before standing up, she hollered, "Get up!" Fumbling amongst the large pile of clothes, I stood and looked up at Mama just as Daddy's shoe hit me across the face. Blood flew from my nose and I flew back into the pile of clothes. Quickly, I curled up, my knees into my chest, my arms up over my head, and silently I started to pray, "Please, dear God, please make Mama stop hitting me. Please don't let her hurt me." Mama told me "Get up! And get me a cup of coffee." As I did, I looked up towards the ceiling and silently said, "Thank you" to God for answering my prayer.

I returned with the coffee. Mama was sitting on the bed, looking down at the floor. I quickly set it down on the night stand and backed away. I was afraid that she was going to throw the scalding coffee on me. It had happened before and it could definitely happen again. Without looking up, Mama warned me to have the pile of clothes ironed and hung up by the time she got out of the shower. Here was my second chance but as I looked at the large pile of clothes, I realized it would be impossible. "Yes, ma'am."

Mama was in the shower when I noticed my nose had bled onto some of the clean clothes. I knew she would kill me if she saw it, so I took the blood stained clothes out to the garage and stuffed them into the washing machine. I figured that I would have the chance to wash them after school and before Mama got home from work. I ran back in and tried to flatten out the much wrinkled clothes. I knew that I wasn't doing my best job at ironing, but I didn't have much time. It seemed to be an impossible job, but I just had a few more to do, then I could change my dress and go to school. I was going to be late, but I was eager to get away from Mama. The water turned off in Mama's bathroom.

Mama walked out of the bathroom naked with a towel around her head. She saw me panicking. That's when she blew up. She told me how stupid I was, and that I was just like my father. She threw on some pants without putting on underwear, then a blouse without a bra. I was still in my new dress from Daddy.

Mama was angry as we got into the car to leave. I thought she was taking me to school. Mama was yelling at me for "...listening to Daddy and not to her." She continued in the car saying that I loved Daddy more than I loved her.

"I love you both the same." I whispered back in defense. I was too afraid to speak louder than a whisper.

"Who do you love more: me or your father?" She asked as she looked straight ahead and continued to drive in the direction of my school. Still in a whisper, I said to her, "I love you both the same." Then Mama started yelling about how I never appreciated anything she did for me and that I didn't appreciate it when she bought me new dresses. She pounded on the dashboard as she drove.

We were just a couple blocks away from school. I felt relieved when I saw the outskirts of the playground. I knew that I would be safe at school, at least for a little while. Then at a stop sign, just one block away from school, Mama hesitated before going straight ahead to school. She looked at me, then down at my bloody dress, and then turned left in the opposite direction. "Oh no," I thought to myself.

"Who do you love more, me or your father?" She yelled as she drove. "I love you both the same." I replied. Gritting her teeth and drawing out each word, "Who do you love _more_? Me or your FATHER?" Then she pulled over, slammed on the brakes, turned toward me and glared as she waited for my reply.

"I love you both the same." I answered. I felt like a whimpering puppy about to get scolded. My head down low, my eyes watery and sincere.

Mama shoved her foot onto the accelerator and we took off. I heard a car slam on the brakes and honk in anger, as Mama pulled out in front of them. Mama blurted out "F--- You!" As she glared at the car behind us in the rear-view mirror, she shook her right fist and raised her middle finger.

I wondered where we were going. At first, I assumed we were going home. But, after a few minutes, I knew that Mama had something else in mind. We went over a narrow bridge that crossed a canal. The canal was off the Manatee River. To my right, there were mangroves. They grew next to a small, man-made brackish lake. To my left was a boat dock. It allowed access to the Manatee River and to the little lake. Mama took a sharp turn to the left into the white shell-laden parking lot of the boat dock. Sand and dust drifted up to the windows as Mama slammed on her brakes.

The commotion had drawn the attention of some construction workers that were busy putting in a new dock about fifty yards away. They stopped and watched us for a second and I thought to myself, "Good, there are people here, I'm safe." Mama didn't put the car in park, instead, she sat there for a second with the engine running. I had no idea what was going on and I wasn't about to ask. "Get out of this f---ing car." Mama said in a stern voice. I didn't move.

"GET OUT!" She screamed without looking at me.
I looked at her with my eyes wide and in an innocent, pleading voice I asked, "Why?"
"Because, I don't <u>want</u> you anymore!" She looked straight into my eyes and said in a low, monstrous voice, "I hate you!" She paused and in that second of silence, I felt my heart, THUMP, THUMP, THUMP. Then she continued, "You love your father more than you love me, and I will hate you for that for the rest of my life."
My heart felt like it was in my throat. "Please Mama, that's not true, please, don't leave me here!"

117

"GET OUT!" She hollered back. "Mama, PLEASE, Don't leave me here! I love you and Daddy both the same." Mama interrupted my loud pleas for forgiveness. She looked at me whimpering in the corner of my seat and said in a calm 'matter of factly' voice, "I'm not going to leave you here." "You're not?" I wiped the tears from my eyes still trying to catch my breath. "No." She replied in a subtle voice, "You're not going to stay here. You're gonna to go up onto that bridge. You're gonna jump off and you're gonna kill yourself!" "Now, get out of this car!" Mama threw the car in park, reached over, opened my door, and pushed me out onto the parking lot made of shells. The shells stuck to the skin on my face and it stung, but it didn't stop me from jumping up and trying to get back into the car. Mama slammed the door shut, locked it and rolled the window up, "Get the f--- up on that bridge!" She said it in a low demanding voice. I tried to open the door and get back into the car. Nervously, I pulled at the handle, pleading softly, "Please, let me in." Mama continued to yell her command to jump off the bridge, and not knowing what to do I hysterically pulled at the door handled, wailing my body back and forth with each tug. I felt as though I was pleading for my life. Begging Mama, I cried out, "Please Mama, please don't make me do this! I don't want to die! Please Mama!" "Who do you love more? Me or your father?" I replied quickly and hysterically, "I love you both the same! Please, let me back in, Mama. I'm scared! Please!"

"I HATE YOU!" Mama blurted out over and over, trying to drown out my pleas to let me into the car. I could feel the sting of the sand on my cheeks and I could taste the dust in my mouth as the tears streamed down my face. This time, softly, I said, "Mama, please, people are watching us. Mama, please let me in the car." I thought maybe that would change her mind. Instead she shook her head wildly, like a dog shaking off water. She used her fist and pounded on the steering wheel. She turned to me, "I don't care! Either you tell me that you love me more than your father, or you go jump off that bridge! Do you understand me, Cheri? Do you love your father enough to kill yourself for him? Do you?" I had been told that people who committed suicide couldn't go to Heaven. I prayed, "God, please don't let me die, please?" I stood there, crying. I looked straight down at the ground, rubbing my hands together, and then, wiping the tears off my cheeks, softly, without looking up, I whimpered back to her, "No ma'am."

"Who do you love more? Me or your Father?"

"Please, Mama, Please Mama don't make me..."

"Who do you love more? Me or your Father?"

With tears streaming down my face, I looked at the sand and whispered, "You."

"Say it. Say it right." She demanded.

Oh God, please let Daddy know that I don't mean this, I thought to myself, as I whispered,   "I love you more, (hesitation) Mama."

Mama reached over, unlocked the door, and finally let me get into the car. She drove me home and told me to change clothes. She called in sick to work, took me to the bar, acted as if nothing ever happened and that's where we spent the rest of the day. Every chance she had, Mama told me over and over, "I love you, Cheri. I really do."

32
"Baby"   November, 1973

I thought it would never be possible but things around our house started feeling like a real home. Mama switched jobs. She quit at Manatee Hospital and started working at another hospital and she was even pleasant to Daddy. She made dinner and didn't argue if Daddy was a little late from work. Every weekend, Mama would get up and make us breakfast. Butch and George weren't early risers, so I would have to go in and jump on them to get them out of bed. They would finally come in and join us. We all sat down at the table. Me in my pajamas, George in his underwear and Butch in cut-offs or whatever he wore to bed the night before. They would eat quickly and go right back to bed. I thought to myself, "Finally, we have a normal family." Daddy even sat at the head of the table and said grace before we ate. I didn't think too much of the sudden change until one day after school Mama let me in on a little secret. She wanted a dog.

Mama worked with a lady whose name was Elizabeth. Mama told me the story that Elizabeth had told her earlier. Elizabeth lived in a trailer and was out on a walk when she heard a puppy whining within a house that she knew was abandoned. The family had been evicted just over a week ago. Hearing the noise, Elizabeth walked up to the house and peered in through the window. There she found the house in shambles. It looked as though it had been vandalized. There was an old torn up couch, ripped curtains and scratch marks all over the front door. As Elizabeth peered in through the window she saw what might have been the culprit of both the damage and the whining. Trotting around the corner of the living room, came a half-grown St. Bernard puppy. Elizabeth ran home, called the police, and together they rescued the dog from the abandoned home. The puppy was then released into Elizabeth's care. Soon, Elizabeth and her husband knew that their trailer couldn't house such a big dog. That's when she asked Mama if she would be interested in a puppy.

Mama was scared to ask Daddy for a dog. Daddy already complained about our two cats, Tomcat and Sneakers (a kitten I had hid in my room for two weeks before Daddy discovered that I had brought it home) eating too much and the gerbil stinking up my bedroom. Mama decided that seeing would be believing. She thought that if she took Daddy over to Elizabeth's house, maybe he would be forced into saying, "Yes."

All month I enjoyed the happiness that existed in our home. Mama's kindness sent a whirlwind of good acts running throughout the family. Daddy came home every night. Butch and George stopped beating each other up for awhile and Mama and I had fun together. She was excited about the puppy and she and I talked and laughed about what it would be like if we could just talk Daddy into letting us keep it. I had never seen a St. Bernard, so Mama took me to the library and we looked one up. Mama read about how much they ate and how big it would get.

Finally the night came that we were supposed to go and see the puppy. Mama still hadn't told Daddy that we had made plans with Elizabeth after dinner. Mama made Daddy's favorite dessert, key lime pie and said, "Lo, tonight we have plans after dinner." Daddy asked, "Oh? What are we doing?" I wanted to blurt out that we were going to look at a puppy, but I knew that if I did, I would spoil everything. I sat at the table waiting to hear what Mama was going to say. "I want you to meet a lady I work with. She's invited us over tonight for a drink." Daddy was totally against it. He was tired and said that Mama and I could go but he didn't want to. Mama begged him, "Please Lo?" That's when I looked at him with my own puppy dog eyes and extended my own.. "Please Daddy?" Daddy reluctantly said that he would go and immediately, I exclaimed in jubilee, "Goodie, Goodie!"

It was on our drive to Elizabeth's trailer that Daddy finally asked what all the excitement was about. Mama was reluctant to tell him, but she finally gave him a quick and short answer, "A puppy." I jumped into the conversation before Daddy could say another word and said, "A ST. BERNARD PUPPY!" Mama turned and gave me a stern look. Daddy, on the other hand, quickly objected to having "a dog that will eat us out of house and home!" We passed by Elizabeth's address and Daddy said that there was no way that he was going to stop. I whined, and Mama said, "You already promised Cheri that you would at least stop by and take a look at it. Besides, I work with Elizabeth and I can't just not show up." Daddy agreed to go into Elizabeth's for five minutes.

We sat on the couch talking for a few minutes as Elizabeth told us the story of how she found Baby. I wondered if she was ever going to bring the puppy out. I was dying to see a real St. Bernard. Then I couldn't believe my eyes. Elizabeth's husband went and let what they were referring to as the "poor little baby" out of the bedroom so that it could come into the living room and greet us. Instead of a "poor little baby" it was a very big baby and it ran into living room looking much like a bull in a china shop. Her drool swooped from side to side as she ran over to us and her tail knocked over glasses that stood on the coffee table. She was adorable. "What's her name?" I asked as I wrapped my arms around her neck, forgetting about her drool. "Baby is her name," Elizabeth answered.

Baby amazingly enough convinced Daddy that she was the dog for him. Daddy was in a chair next to the couch and after I released her from my hug, she turned to Daddy. Daddy gave her two inexpressive pats on the head and tried to shoo her off to Mama, but Baby wanted more. As Daddy turned her around to face Mama, she backed right around and jumped up onto Daddy's lap. Baby was much too big to be a lap dog, so half her body hung off the chair. Mama chuckled, "Lo, I think she likes you." Then Mama turned to Elizabeth and made a joke, "He always did have a way with women." Everyone laughed and that night we brought Baby home with us.

33
Christmas Eve

My parents always made me go to bed early on Christmas Eve. I would lie there in bed and try to fall asleep wondering what I would find out under the Christmas tree the next day. There were many times that I was very frightened that I wouldn't find anything at all. Mama told me often that if I didn't "start being a good girl," Santa would not come at all to our house. I prayed to God and told Him how sorry I was for not being a better listener. I confessed everything that I had ever done wrong. I dozed off as I prayed.

Christmas 1973

I woke up before it was even light outside. I was so excited I ran out of my room and into the living room where our Christmas tree stood. In amazement, I stood there as the glee of Christmas morning fell from my face. Santa didn't come to my house, Mama was right. Tears filled my eyes and I didn't know what to do. I tapped on my parent's door but they didn't hear me. I was scared to storm into their room. I walked over to the garage door and went outside into the cold damp garage. There lay Baby. She came over to soothe my aching heart as I sat telling her how sorry I was for forgetting to feed her all those times. She didn't seem very mad. She had already forgiven me. I was sure that God had forgiven me too. I sat there crying as I asked God, "Why? Why is it me who always has to be punished?" Finally, I gathered up my

125

strength and went into Mama and Daddy's room. I woke up Daddy and told him the bad news.

"Daddy, wake up. Santa Claus forgot me."

Daddy was groggy, "What?" He asked in a confused voice.

"Daddy, Santa didn't come. I'm so sad."

"Cheri, What time is it?"

"I don't know."

"Daddy looked up at the clock and was irritated that I woke him up. "Cheri, it's the middle of the night. Santa has a lot of places to go. I'm sure he's coming, he just isn't here yet. Now go back to bed."

"But, Daddy, Mama told me if I was bad, then..."

"Cheri, trust me. Go back to bed and go to sleep. Santa will come."

I went back to bed and cried myself to sleep knowing that Daddy didn't understand.

The next morning, Mama came into my room. "Aren't you gonna get out of bed, sleepy head? Don't you want to see what Santa brought?"

At first, I looked at Mama quite bewildered. Didn't she know that Santa had forgotten me? Then I remembered what Daddy said about Santa having a lot of places to go. It took less than a second for me to jump out of bed and run into our Florida room. There beneath our artificial Christmas tree were many unwrapped presents from Santa. My heart was filled with jubilation! Santa hadn't forgotten me after all.

34
Where's Daddy?   January, 1974

Mama was a good nurse at work and at home she wasn't any different. Whenever I was at home sick she would always make me feel better. She would lay out a blanket on the Florida room floor for me and let me play dolls or color as I watched television. Being sick also meant that she would make me soup and a sandwich, and treat me like a very special little girl.

One day, I stayed home from school and things went well until a little after supper time. Mama was upset because it was another one of those days that Daddy decided not to come home. She called every bar in town looking for Daddy. Sometimes, Mama would hand me the phone and I would have to ask for Daddy. Mama had called the bars so much that the bartenders recognized her voice and would say that Daddy wasn't there even if he really was.

That day, Mama couldn't find Daddy anywhere so she gathered up the boys and me and we went out to find him. We checked every hot spot that Daddy would usually stop at. Mama would make the boys go in to the bar and look for Daddy. If they didn't see him they would have to ask the bartender if he had been there, what time he left and who he left with. The boys hated it. Mama knew all the places that Daddy like to drink. Once, when Mama found Daddy's car in a bar parking lot, she made George siphon the gas out of Daddy's tank and into her own gas tank. Then she left an unfriendly note on his windshield as to how he could call a cab to get home.

Mama was getting increasingly furious as she drove around and couldn't find a trace of Daddy. She finally concluded that he was at some other woman's house. She was mad and taking it out on everything and everyone that stepped in her way. She wanted revenge on Daddy and decided to go to Ray's, "Just to calm her nerves," she said. Butch and George, now in high school, did not want to go to a run-down bar with their mother. They refused to go and threatened to walk home if she didn't drop them off. Home was on the other side of town and Mama wasn't going to drive all the way back home. She was frustrated and yelled at them about the price of gas. All I wanted to do was go home to bed. I had stayed home sick from school and I still didn't feel well. I was tired, achy and had a bad cough. Mama was sick of our whining and decided to drop us off at Grandma California's house. My cough was getting increasingly worse. Grandma lived just about six blocks from the Tropicana® orange juice plant and we were at the corner of Tropicana®. I coughed again. I had coughed during the entire search for Daddy. Now, Mama was furious with Daddy, frustrated with the boys and irritated with my continuos cough.

"If you cough one more time, I am going to turn around and make you regret it. Do you understand me, Cheri?" I suddenly sat back in my seat and slouched low so that if she reached over to slap me, most of her hand would miss me, "Yes ma'am." I whispered back.

Breathing through my mouth I could feel the congestion all the way down into my lungs. It felt as though I could hardly breathe at all. How was I going to stop coughing? Thinking about how not to cough made me want to cough even more. Mama turned towards Grandma's house. We were only three blocks away. I decided the only thing to do was to hold my breath. I took as deep of a breath as I could and held it in. Mama stopped at the stop sign. We were two blocks away from

Grandma's. She decided to light a cigarette. She sat at the stop sign digging through her purse and waiting for the lighter to pop out of the dashboard. I thought to myself, "Hurry up. I can't hold it very much longer." Mama looked in the rearview mirror at me as she lit her cigarette. My cheeks were puffed out and she could tell that I was holding my breath. Slowly she put the car in gear but I couldn't hold my breath any longer. I felt like I was going to explode! So as I took a breath of air, soft, and quiet as I could...I coughed. Mama had just crossed the intersection when she slammed on the brakes, one block from Grandma's house.

Mama turned around, "Didn't I tell you not to cough?" She reached over the seat and before she could hit me I yelled out, "I couldn't help it Mama, I'm sorry!"

Mama slapped my leg and screamed, "Didn't I tell you not to cough? You little brat, you never listen to anything I say!" She put the cigarette in her mouth and leaned over the seat. She proceeded to hit me on the thighs, the shoulders, the head, anywhere her hand would reach. George scooted over close to the window out of reach of Mama. Butch, finally fed up with the entire ordeal, stormed out of the car and slammed the car door shut. He headed for Grandma's and Mama turned around and drove fast ahead to beat him there. As we stopped in front of the house Grandma met us at the door. Mama started crying about how bad us kids were and how Daddy was sleeping around on her. She said that nobody cared about her. Grandma generously suggested that the boys and I stay with her. Mama asked Grandma if she could borrow a couple of dollars to stop and get a pack of cigarettes and a beer. Grandma reached into her bra and pulled out a few dollars and handed them over to Mama. Mama thanked her and quickly disappeared out the   door.

Light Beyond the Darkness

35
Something We Did Every Day

Some of the neighborhood kids and I built a fort in my back yard. When it wasn't being used by the neighborhood kids, I used it as my hiding spot. It sounds funny, but it was easy to hide in my own back yard. All I had to do was go in and tune out the fighting, tune out the drinking, tune out all the bad stuff. I would cover my ears and just smell the freshness of the orange trees that grew in our back yard.

One day while I was out in the fort, some friends stopped by and we sat inside and talked. They decided that I should be treasurer of the fort. It was a great feeling to be elected to such an important role. I felt needed and loved. I felt good.

Under the chatter of our conversation, I heard a familiar sound. I heard Mama and Daddy arguing. I could tell that the noise was coming from their open window and I sat there praying that no one else would hear it. I was embarrassed. I was also afraid; not because my parents were fighting, but for my popularity. What if my friends heard Mama cussing at Daddy and decided that I wasn't good enough to be treasurer. Half of me wanted to go in and tell them to stop fighting. Didn't they know that they were embarrassing me? Didn't they care that my friends could hear them? The other half of me didn't want to go in; I was too scared. I knew if I interrupted their fight, they would get mad at me and then I definitely wouldn't be able to go back outside. It was a losing battle. With all my concentration on what I should do, I didn't even notice if my friends had heard them or not. Before I even had a chance to say anything,

George was knocking at the clubhouse door. "Cheri, you need to come in the house now. Your friends should probably go home too." I didn't even argue. I was embarrassed and just wanted to crawl out and die. As George and I walked in the house I asked him what was going on. "We have to take Mama to the hospital." He said it as if it were something we did every day. "Why?" I asked, knowing that it had to be related to their fight. "Dad broke her arm."

I ran in the house and back to our parents' bedroom, stopping for a second in the dining room only to notice that it was in shambles. Chairs were thrown all over and one was smashed into pieces. In the wall I saw what I dreaded the most: knife marks. I knew immediately that Mama had tried to stab Daddy again.

Mama was crying as she sat on her bed holding her arm. "What happened?" I asked.
"Look what your father did to me?" Mama replied as she held out her arm to show me. As she looked up at me I noticed her mascara had streaked her face.
Her arm was grotesquely disfigured. The bones between her wrist and elbow were broken in half. One had just barely punctured the skin. Mama had been sipping beers all day and that probably helped numb the pain. But I knew it hurt. I could tell by her trembling voice. She cried, "Isn't he terrible Cheri? How could he do this to me?" She wanted to be comforted. She needed me to tell her how terrible Daddy was to have broken her arm. I stood there for a moment staring at her arm. It made me sick to my stomach. I looked at her face. Something inside me wanted to comfort her, but all I could do was stand there. Pictures of Daddy raced through my mind. Pictures of blood pouring over the sidewalk as it ran from his back. I remembered his nose ripped opened as though it were an envelope. I stood there, selfishly thinking that Mama probably got what she deserved. I turned around and called out to George, "You better take Mama to the

hospital <u>now</u>." I left her room. I told George I didn't want to go to the hospital. I had stayed home many times before alone, and I could do it again. George didn't approve but didn't feel like arguing with me. So he left. Several hours later he returned alone. They had to keep Mama in the hospital overnight. Mama was having major surgery and had to have a metal plate put in her arm.

Then, and only then, did I feel guilty for not showing more compassion to Mama. I had a chance to help her, and I didn't. A part of me wanted revenge for all the terrible things she had done to me, and not being compassionate was my revenge. Why didn't it feel as good as I thought it would? Why did I feel so guilty? I should have felt avenged, but for some reason I felt like I did something terribly wrong.

Romans 12: 17-21 (TLB)

Never pay back evil for evil. Do things in such a way that everyone can see you are honest clear through. Don't quarrel with anyone. Be at peace with everyone, just as much as possible.

Dear friends, never avenge yourselves. Leave that to God, for he has said that he will repay those who deserve it. (Don't take the law into your own hands.) Instead, feed your enemy if he is hungry. If he is thirsty give him something to drink and you will be "heaping coals of fire on his head." In other words, he will feel ashamed of himself for what he has done to you. Don't let evil get the upper hand but conquer evil by doing good.

Later, I found out that Daddy made a promise to Mama many years ago; he warned her that if she ever came after him with a knife again he would kill her. That afternoon, when Mama and Daddy were fighting Mama tried three times to stab Daddy with a fillet knife. Mama missed and stabbed the wall all three times. That explained the three knife holes in the wall. Daddy was angry and he tried several times to warn her to put the knife down. They fought in the dining room around the table. That explained the messed up chairs. Finally, when Mama tried to stab Daddy again, he picked up a chair and slammed it down on Mama's arm.

36
The Underground Fort

They built a few more houses in our neighborhood. One family moved in two houses down from us, with four children: three girls and a boy. They had a swimming pool, and we played together a lot. Gabrielle, their eldest daughter, was a year older than me. She taught me to do back flips off the side of the pool. I spent many nights at their house. Gabe gave me a book to read. It was about "warm fuzzies." It talked about how you have to love yourself and that you get "warm fuzzies" from people who are kind to you. Gabe always seemed concerned about me and my family. She was a great friend to talk to. Together, she, her sister Liz, who was my age but very shy, and I got all the neighborhood kids together to build a new fort. Daddy made the boys tear down the other fort because one day I came home and told him a joke that I didn't understand. An older boy had told me the joke the day before in the fort. When I repeated it to Daddy, he got angry and said that I couldn't repeat it. Then he made the boys take every board out of my fort.

We dug a huge hole in the lot next to her house. It was going to be an underground fort. It was about ten feet by ten feet and about five feet deep. It took many days and a few injuries to complete the hole.

Every day after school I ran over with my shovel to do my share of digging. One day, I had on a brand new pair of shoes that Mama had bought me. I didn't want my new shoes to get full of sand so I took them off before running across the warm white sand to start my digging.

135

We were less than ten miles from the beach and so our dirt was black. It was sandy colored. As the sun beat down, the sand began to heat up like a burner on the stove, and soon it was too hot for my feet to tolerate. I buried my feet about three inches from the surface where the sand remained cool and soothing, and then continued to dig. Later, I looked up and saw Daddy walking over. I was nervous because I figured he wanted to see what we were doing. I thought he might be mad that we were building a new fort. I began to shovel faster, partly nervous and partly, showing off that I could shovel so well. I totally forgot that my feet were hidden about shoulder's width apart under the sand. As Daddy approached, I decided to secure my shovel into the ground next to me. Gripping the handle, I raised it about a foot off the ground and slammed it straight into the sand <u>and</u> right into my foot! Owww! I sprang out of the sand, staining it with blood, as Daddy came over and asked me what in the world was I thinking. How could I tell him that I was trying to impress him? How could I explain that I was afraid Mama would be mad at me if I got my new shoes dirty? I just said, "I don't know."

Daddy carried me home and washed my foot in the garage sink. He promised not to tell Mama what happened, because he knew if she found out, she wouldn't let me play in the fort anymore.

37
A Real Lesson With Piano   August, 1973

Since we attended church up in Sanford, I had wanted to play the piano. My goal was to take lessons so that when I was old, I could play the piano in church. I would sit at our piano that I had gotten for my ninth birthday, and pretend to play beautiful hymns.

Mama asked me if I still wanted to take piano lessons. Mama knew that I wanted to take lessons. I guess we just couldn't afford them because she never signed me up for them. But I think she really wanted me to take lessons so she continued to ask. This time when she asked me I told her yes and then I proceeded to tell her <u>why</u> I wanted lessons.

Mama loved church and I guess the thought of her daughter playing the piano on Sundays was enough to convenience her that it was time. Mama called around and found a little old lady to teach me. At first I really loved it. I practiced everyday. Then I decided that practicing just wasn't that fun. When I realized that it was going to take hard work to play that piano, my dreams started to fade. I figured that I was young and that I could always learn to play later, when I got older. However, Mama wouldn't let me quit. She made me practice that piano every single day for a half hour. I couldn't do anything after school until I sat down and practiced that piano. There were days that I cried and thought that she was the meanest person in the world. I wondered how she could deprive me of playing with my friends and instead she kept me inside at that old piano.

The older I became the more grateful I became of her persistence. She taught me to work for what I wanted, not to lose sight of my dreams, and that not everything in life came easy. She taught me that I couldn't just give up. It was a good lesson in life and has paid off in more than just playing the piano. From the day I started playing the piano, I wound up taking lessons for almost fourteen years. I also went on to play the tuba and French horn in junior and senior high school band.

37
Walking in Darkness   September, 1974

*"Sometimes it takes a walk in complete darkness, to teach
us to walk in the light."*
Author unknown

One day Mama and I drove out of Bradenton, into
the woods to visit a friend of Mama's. We drove to a
place called Linger Lodge®. We had to travel east from
Bradenton into the country to get to Linger Lodge®. The
road we traveled upon was narrow and bumpy. Like
many of the country roads in Florida, there were ditches
on either side of the road. Beyond the shallow ravines
that were filled with water, lay rows and rows of tall
evergreen trees. I sat in the passenger seat, staring out
the window. I sat there staring at the rows and rows of
tall, green, trees. They were planted many years ago in
straight lines.

As Mama drove and sang to the radio, I sat staring,
daydreaming the entire time. Then something caught my
attention. It was a big, orange and white billboard by the
side of the road. It read "LINGER LODGE." It had an
arrow that pointed to the right. Mama slowed as we
approached the sign and followed the arrow. We drove
upon a wide dirt road and curved around its many
corners. It seemed to take us a long time to get from the
sign to Linger Lodge®. Once we got closer, I could see
that Linger Lodge® was a trailer court. To our left were
all sorts of trailers, some more attractive than others. It
appeared that some had made Linger Lodge their
permanent home. I wondered how anyone could live so
far out in the country. To the back of the trailer court

was a small, white house with an eight foot tall fence around the yard. Across the dirt road from the little house was a large, brick building. Mama said that the building held a bar, grocery store, and game room. Behind the brick building was the part that interested me the most, for back there lay paths that extended down to a small canal. Residents and guests of Linger Lodge® could swim in a restricted area, fish, or canoe through the winding canals in search of alligators or better fishing spots.

Mama and I drove out to Linger Lodge® so that Mama could see a guy that she had met at a bar in Bradenton. His name was Tracy, and he lived with another guy named Mike. Mama had only seen him a couple times and wanted to make a good impression. She was wearing a dark red dress that outlined her soft figure. The hem line was above her knee. The V-neck outlined Mama's breasts and showed her bra when she purposely bent over to adjust her red, high heels. Though Mama looked stunning with her jet black hair swept up off her neck, she looked very out of place for Linger Lodge®. A place where people go to relax, fish, swim and enjoy mostly outdoor activities.

By the time we found Tracy's place, it was starting to get cloudy, and I knew it was going to rain soon. Tracy gave us a quick tour of the trailer court and the path that led down to the water. The little, white, house had peacocks and rabbits that ran freely in the fenced-in yard. I could have stood there and watched them for hours, but Mama was eager to go into the bar. She didn't want her hair to get wet by the sprinkles that were starting to come down faster and harder. Mama and Tracy decided to have a beer while we waited for the sprinkles to stop. Though I didn't ask for anything, Tracy bought me a coke and some chips. I looked at Mama to make sure that it was okay to accept the generous gift, and Mama nodded yes.

The bar was a relatively large building compared to the trailers. It contained one long counter which served as the bar. Behind the counter was a large selection of food and drink. The other area contained two pool tables, some pinball machines, and a couch and fireplace. Mama and Tracy sat at the bar and drank while I played pool. The time went slowly for me. Mama gave me a few quarters, and I had to make them last. I entertained myself with the various games throughout the bar. I could hear the rain as it hit the windows. I sat down on the couch in front of the window. I could see the path that led to the water. The tall, green trees shaded out what little light had made it through the thick, dark, gray clouds. It looked mysterious, intriguing, and yet innocent. As I sat there, I had to drown out the background of chatter of the bar and thought about living alone out in the vast solitude of the trees and nature. The very thought seemed quaint, and peaceful.
(I started this poem during that day and finished the second verse shortly after that night.)

> *I want to sit in a world of darkness*
> *and see beyond the walls,*
> *all my senses lose their larkness*
> *and follow God's dreams and calls.*
>
> *To hear not one scream or holler,*
> *only laughter filled with tears,*
> *And God's full creations*
> *filling love within my ears.*

Tracy interrupted my daydreaming to ask me to play a game of pool. I could tell that he felt sorry for me. I looked at Mama. She looked cross. She was angry about something. I wondered whether it was something that I had done? I nodded to Tracy that I would play. I didn't say much to Tracy as we played; instead, I continued to

141

keep an eye on Mama. As soon as Tracy won the game, I said, "Thank you" and ran over to Mama. She wouldn't look at me. I tapped her on the leg, and asked, "Mama, can I go outside and play for a little while...please?" She seemed relieved to get me out of the bar.

I ran out to the car, grabbed my raincoat and started out to the back of the building. First, I played in the wooded paths, searching the way down to the water. As I played along the path, I continued to look back at the windows of the bar. Where it had seemed friendly and inviting before, it was now scary being on the path all alone. The trees shadowed the sky, making it darker than usual and the drizzle made it dreary. Finally, I made it to the sandy, wet beach, and there in the open, I felt safe and secure. I played for hours in the sand, pretending to be shipwrecked. My clothes were already wet when I pushed the canoe that laid beside the beach halfway into the water. I sat in it, pretending to be an explorer in search of alligators. The rain had almost stopped, and I sat watching the water. My eyes were searching for signs of life, a sign of an alligator surfacing.

"Cheri! Cheri! Time to come back now!" It startled me to hear Mama's voice. I jumped out of the canoe and looked up towards the bar. I couldn't see anyone, in fact, because of the shady trees, I couldn't even see the bar. That's when I noticed it was almost dark. I pulled the canoe out of the water and ran for the path. I took a few steps and realized that I didn't know where the path was anymore. It was getting too dark and I was afraid that if I went in much farther that I would get lost. Mama continued to call for me. I could tell she was getting angry. I was too scared to take the path, and yet I was too scared of Mama getting mad at me to stay. I was confused, so, I ran back to the beach, crying frantically and falling to my knees in the sand. I sat there crying, listening to Mama scream out my name. Should I call back to her? Would she be mad at me if she found me?

Weakly, I hollered out, "Mama? Mama? I'm down here." Within minutes I could hear Mama and Tracy following the path. I was scared that Mama would be mad if I was just sitting on the beach waiting for them, so I went over to the edge of the path and slowly started up. I was glad that Tracy was with Mama because I felt safer with Mama when other people were around. We met on the path not far from the beach. Mama interrogated me as to why I didn't come when she called for me the first time. Interrupting Mama, Tracy asked, "Are you okay?" I nodded, thinking to myself how good it felt for someone to be worried about me. I looked at Mama. Her hair was wet from the rainwater dripping down from the trees. Under her eyes were dark, black smudges, and she was holding her red, high heels in her right hand. I told Mama that I was too scared to go back up the path. Mama told me it wasn't a good enough excuse, and then she said, "You just wait till you get home, young lady."

Tracy and Mama led me back up to the bar. Mama went into the bathroom and freshened up as Tracy and I ordered a pizza from the bar. I was starving. Mama wouldn't let me play any more of the games in the bar, so I lay down on an old couch by the fireplace. Laying there, my teeth chattering from the chill of the rain and my wet clothes, I fell asleep.

It was late when Mama finally woke me up, and I could tell by the way she spoke that she had had too much to drink. The three of us walked back to Tracy's trailer, and Mama tried to gather her things to leave. I was scared to ride home with Mama. It was late and I was afraid that Mama wouldn't be able to drive. "Mama, are you sure you can drive?" I asked, knowing that I was stepping out of my boundaries. Tracy interrupted and suggested that we stay overnight. Mama said that Daddy would kill her if she didn't get home. Tracy said, "Okay then, stay here on the couch for a few hours, get some rest, and sleep off some of those beers you had." I agreed

143

with Tracy, saying that I would rather stay for a little while. Tracy took Mama's keys and said he would give them back after she rested. Mama was angry, and she started undressing right there in the living room in front of Tracy and me. I was embarrassed. Tracy cleared his throat and then turned around with his back to Mama. She stripped down to her bra and underwear and walked around the trailer, opening closets and doors, looking for a pillow. Tracy explained to Mama, "Carol, why don't you have a seat on the couch. Mike's in the back bedroom, and I wouldn't want him to see you this way." Mama budged by Tracy and walked to the back bedroom, opened the door and said in a drunken slur, "Hi, Mike, I'm Carol. Tracy was too embarrassed to introduce us earlier." Then she slammed the door, turned around and came back into the living room. Tracy was in the hall getting blankets and pillows as Mike came out of the bedroom. "Everything's okay, Mike. Carol's just had a little too much to drink." Tracy assured Mike, sending him back to watch television in his bedroom.

Tracy left Mama's keys on the counter before he headed to bed. Tracy had one couch in his living room, and Mama and I both slept on it that night. Mama passed out quickly. It was still dark out when I awoke. At first, I didn't know what was going on. I felt sharp pains in my side and I thought that I was having a dream. Instead, I was awakening into a nightmare.

Mama stood beside the couch. I opened my eyes just as her right leg came up and kicked me in the side just below my ribs. OWWW! Why was Mama kicking me? I thought to myself, "This must be a dream." I opened my eyes and tried to focus on what was happening. It was apparent when I felt the blow of another kick. This one nailed me in my ribs on the left side.

Mama spoke softly with her teeth gritted. She was still wearing only her bra and underwear, and her hair was thrown around her head like a rat's nest. "You f---ed him didn't ya?" Before I could say a word, Mama kicked me again in my left side. "You went in his bedroom while I was asleep and f---ed him, didn't you?" I sat up and then stood as I tried to defend myself from Mama. "You f--ked him, didn't you?" Defenselessly I tried to answer, "I don't know what you're talking about, Mama. I've been asleep right here." Mama interrupted, "SHH!"

At the same time, her fist smashed against my jaw and ear, knocking me back onto the couch. "You little liar. You f---ed him. I heard you. Don't ever lie to me!" I pleaded with her, "Mama, I don't understand what you mean. Please, tell me what you mean. Why are you mad at me?"
Mama told me to stand up but I was too scared to move.
"Get up," Mama told me again. I cried as I slowly pushed myself up off the couch. My stomach and sides hurt as my body attempted to stand straight.

"Shut up and stop your crying." Mama reached out and grabbed my arm, pulled me close to her and squeezed the back of my arm hard. She whispered the threat into my face, "I'll kill you if you wake them up." Quietly I replied, "Ouch, you're hurting me." Mama let go. She moved over to the couch and took off two of the cushions. I stood back, wondering what she was doing and at the same time, praying silently, "Help me understand. Oh God, what did I do? What is Mama talking about? Oh God, Why is she mad at me? Please, Dear God, don't let her hurt me anymore! Please?!"

I couldn't believe my ears. Mama had pulled off the cushions and was throwing up <u>in</u> the couch. "Mama? Mama, are you okay?" She turned to me, "Shh! Shut up." She was still drunk. Once she had finished vomiting, she put the cushions back on the couch as though nothing had ever happened. She lay down and fell back to sleep. I sat in the recliner across from the couch. First, I thanked God for making

145

Mama go back to sleep and leaving me alone. Then I curled up in the chair. I sat there scared and wondered what Mama would do next. Silent tears rolled down my cheeks as I laid my head on the arm of the chair and dozed off into a light sleep.

As soon as I heard Mama stir, I woke up and sat up in the chair. I didn't want to be caught off guard again. Mama woke up, looked around the room and told me to get ready to go. After Mama put on her alcohol-stained dress and shoes, we went out to her car. I put my raincoat and my wet shoes in the back seat and then sat in the front seat next to Mama. I could tell that Mama didn't feel good and I was scared about the long ride home.

"So, when did you and Tracy plan all this out?" Mama asked inquisitively as she sped out of the driveway and down the dirt road. "Plan what Mama?" I replied. Mama backhanded me in the mouth as she yelled out, "Don't lie to me!" I could taste blood, and I felt my lip beginning to swell up. "I know you f---ed that son-of-a bit-h. I should have killed him, that's what I should have done." With my hand up to my mouth, I knew Mama would get mad if I didn't answer, yet I didn't know what to say. With tears in my eyes, I whispered, "I'm sorry Mama, but I slept on the couch the whole time. I didn't do anything. I don't even know what you're talking about."

Mama slammed on the brakes and I slid forward hitting the dashboard. I started crying, mostly out of fright.

"That will teach you not to put your seat belt on! Now, get the f--k out of this car. I hate your stupid little as-."

I only looked at Mama and thought to myself, "Oh please don't do this to me." With tears running down my cheeks, I sat there not knowing what to say to her.

Mama repeated, "Get out of this f--king car!" Mama reached down, took off her high heel, and started hitting me with it. She was completely out of control.

"Ouch, Mama, that hurts, Ouch. Ouch, Mama!"

"GET OUT OF THIS CAR, NOW!" She screamed at the top of her lungs.

With my right hand on the door handle and my left arm up trying to block Mama's shots, I cried out, "Why, Mama? Why are you going to leave me?"

Continuing to hit me with her shoe, she said, "You f---ing slut, you slept with the only guy I liked. You f---ed him right in front of me! Now, GET OUT OF THIS CAR!"

I opened the door and got out of the car. Mama drove off as fast as she could, leaving me on the dark, deserted road.

I stood wiping the dust out of my eyes, trying to stop crying as I caught a glimpse of her taillights disappear around a curve. I could hear her driving away. All around me it was pitch black. "Oh God, what should I do?" I muttered over and over as I spoke to God in a soft prayer. "Why me? Oh God, why me? Why does Mama hate me so? What in the world is she talking about? Just tell me what I did wrong."

It was quiet except for the whistle of the trees and the rustling of the branches. The rain had stopped. I was frightened. I started to walk in the same direction that Mama had gone and as I walked I prayed that she would come back to get me. In my bare feet, I walked along the wet dirt road crying, when a comforting song came to me and I whispered the words, "Jesus loves me, this I know..." The words were broken from my tears and cracking voice. The longer I walked the easier it was to see. After what seemed forever, but was more likely fifteen to twenty minutes, I reached the paved road. As I stepped out onto the pavement, I saw Mama's car, sitting idle. Mama was standing outside the car, vomiting in the ditch beside the road. I ran up, "Are you okay, Mama?" Mama looked up, wiped her mouth, and just said, "Get in the car." As soon as I got in the car, I put on my seat belt and then thanked God for making Mama wait for me. Mama said very few words to me for the rest of the trip home.

The only thing she said about Tracy was that she thought he and Mike were gay. After asking what she meant, I thought about it for the rest of the trip home. I didn't want to judge Tracy or Mike. Tracy showed concern for Mama and me by not letting her drive drunk so no matter what Mama said, I decided he was a nice person.

We pulled into our driveway just as the sun was coming up. As we walked into the house, Daddy opened the bedroom door. I could tell that he was mad. Mama told me to go into my bedroom. As I walked away, relieved to be home, I heard Daddy in an angry voice ask where we were. They were arguing before I even shut my bedroom door. As I lay down that morning to try and sleep, I looked up to the ceiling, "Oh God, will this ever end? Do I have to live in this nightmare for the rest of my life? I would rather die."

Little did I know what affect all those harsh words from Mama would have on my life. After meeting a pastor who studied spiritual warfare, I discovered that we can curse people with our tongues. The curse causes us to fall into bondage. Bondage is the foothold we give Satan. There are three types of bondage; lineage from our ancestors, such as alcoholism, gambling, stealing, etc, our own sins is the second type of bondage, and finally, witchcraft and curses. By telling someone they are lazy, or stupid, we place over their head an expectation and often a curse in which that person will live up to until they realize the power they can have through Jesus Christ. I thank the Lord that we have the power through Christ to break those harm-filled statements, to ask for forgiveness for our own sins and to break our lineage that gives Satan a foothold in our lives. We are cleaned through the blood of Christ, but we must seek first forgiveness, then bind the strong man and take back what Christ has given us. For more information I would refer anyone to read Neal Anderson's The Bondage Breaker.

38
Grandma's Surprise   December, 1974

Christmas time. In our family we had one Christmas tradition; Santa came and we opened presents Christmas morning. I knew that Christmas was the celebration of the birth of Jesus Christ but our family didn't talk much about it. Mama would sometimes mention it here and there, but we celebrated more with Santa and giving gifts. At this time, I knew that Santa didn't exist, yet I pretended that I <u>did</u> believe in him. I pretended for Mama's sake. I was afraid of disappointing her. She received so much happiness in giving. I didn't want to take away those few precious moments that Mama had in watching me jump for joy over the wonders that lay under our tree. She truly loved giving.

That year instead of putting our artificial tree in the Florida room, we put it in the living room. I liked helping Mama decorate the tree. Mama and I also picked out imitation leather jackets for Butch and George at the Eagle Army Navy Store®. They were identical jackets and I couldn't wait to see them on the boys.

Christmas day, we went over to see Grandma California and Grandpa. We bought Grandma chocolate and underwear. For Grandpa, we bought a carton of cigarettes. When we got to their house there was a note on the door. The note was a poem written by Grandma. It had five different colored strings attached to it that led into the house. The poem said that each person in my family was to follow a different colored string and at the end of the string was a surprise. I thought it was the greatest! I followed my string from the porch to the living room. I followed it all through the house and finally, in my Grandma's top dresser drawer, I found a present all wrapped in red. It was a great way to receive a gift and I felt very special. It wasn't <u>what</u> the gift was that was so important; it was the thought that Grandma California had put into the gift that made it so special to me. Grandma and Grandpa didn't have much money, yet in a very special way they showed us that they cared.

39

Daddy's Tears   April, 1975

After school one Friday afternoon, Mama got an idea that she thought would be humorous. It was, in a sense, revenge against Daddy. Little did I know that her idea would affect me for the rest of my life. We went home and got a pair of Daddy's boxer underwear. Mama said that she was going to pay Daddy back for all the times he had stopped at the bar and lied to her. Mama and I drove out to the power plant where Daddy was working. It was early afternoon. Mama drove up to the only exit of the plant and told me to get out of the car and help her find a couple of sticks. I got out and together we found two medium width sticks that were about two feet long. Mama shoved the sticks into the ground. I didn't understand the plan until Mama stretched the legs of Daddy's underwear across the two sticks. Daddy was a big man but his boxers looked even bigger stretched between the sticks. I giggled as I looked at the unusual sight standing at the only exit from Daddy's work. Innocently, I thought it would be funny for everyone to see Daddy's. Mama knew that unless there was some sort of sign near the underwear, no one would know who they belonged to. So Mama grabbed part of a box and, with red lipstick, she wrote:

FOOT'S FAT AS-

Foots was a nick-name Daddy was labeled with when his coworkers and friends noticed his shoe size (size 16EEE).

Everything was fun and games until Daddy arrived home that night. I thought he would laugh at

Mama's joke. Instead, I felt his pain through the look in his eyes.

When his car pulled up into the driveway, I ran up to the door to greet him with a smile. Mama, on the other hand, locked herself in her room. She seemed a little frightened and perhaps unsure of what she had done. When I opened the door for Daddy, my smile vanished. Daddy had tears streaking down his dirt-ridden cheeks and in his left hand he carried the two sticks and his underwear.

"What's the matter, Daddy?" I asked. As Daddy looked down at me, I saw that his soft blue eyes were swollen and red. He stared with disappointment at my own blue eyes. I knew at that moment, I had hurt Daddy again. I knew that look too well. He didn't answer me. He went to the bedroom door and attempted to open it. Finding it locked he said, "I hope you're happy. I worked late and was the last one to leave the plant. Every one of the men who work for me saw this," and then he threw the sign and underwear on the carpet. "I have never been so embarrassed in my life. Carol, how could you do this to me?"

I never intended to hurt Daddy, and I felt ashamed for my actions. I had even laughed as Mama and I planted that terrible trap for Daddy. I had laughed at what caused Daddy great pain and embarrassment.

40
Please Don't Die Mama!

Mama got depressed often. She would tell us that she wanted to die. Her famous words were "Nobody loves me." My brothers and I knew that was our cue to say, "Yes, we do Mama, we all love you." There were times that we would have to sit for hours and listen to Mama and affirm our love for her. This happened so often that after a while we began to sound like robots with expressionless voices, telling Mama what she wanted to hear. Off and on, Mama would taking a drug called Valium, and I wasn't sure if it had anything to do with it, but when she drank and took her pills she would almost always attempt or threaten suicide. The first few times it really scared me when Mama threatened to cut her wrist or blow her brains out. After a while I became cold to it just like Butch and George. They said it was a cry for attention. Mama had a desire to be the center of attention. Maybe she was lonely because Daddy and the boys were gone most of the time. I tried to be away a lot too, but I wasn't as successful as the boys and Daddy. However, with everyone away Mama knew just where to go to get attention: the bar.

When Mama and I were home alone, I often went outside. Either I would just sit and pet Tomcat or Baby, or I would play in the field next to our house. I had a vivid imagination and often could pretend to be stranded or living on my own. It was one of those afternoons that Mama called me from my make-believe happy world and told me that we were gonna go to the bar.

153

When we arrived at the bar, I could tell that all Mama wanted was a little attention. I felt sorry for her. She tried desperately to get noticed but no one paid much attention to her. She was unhappy on the inside and it showed on the outside. The more she drank and the less she got noticed, the angrier she became. There began the vicious cycle of her depression; she started out lonely, she got drunk, then angry and then even more lonely.

That night after leaving the bar we went home. George was at home so I warned him that I thought Mama was pretty mad. Of course, it was common for Mama to be upset after coming home from the bar, so I explained to George that Mama was threatening suicide in the car and this time, I thought she may really try to do it. George had heard the "suicide story" so many times that it just didn't faze him anymore. He turned and asked, "What do you want me to do?" I didn't know, so I just said, "Maybe we should just stay with her or talk to her?"

George and I sat by Mama's bed as she cried. She lay there in bed telling us how bad of a husband Daddy was to her and what a terrible childhood she had. She told us of how her father beat her because she looked like her mother. She told us about the time when she was less than six years old and her mother abandoned her and her younger sister for almost four days. Mama had to go to the neighbor's house and ask for bread to eat. Once she was given bread or any kind of food, she would divide it with her sister and with water from the faucet they survived. Envy and jealously arose in Mama as she spoke about how her sister, Marilyn, was never beaten like she was.

George grew tired of what he thought was just another act of attention and left the room to watch television. Mama continued. She expressed her unattainable dreams about being an RN. She changed the subject to God and told me that God put everyone one earth for a purpose. She didn't know why God wanted her to suffer so much. She said the only good thing that she ever had was us kids. She loved us kids more than anything. All she ever wanted, she told me, was for us kids to have a good life. I felt all joked up inside. I never realized that Mama and I had the same hope of happiness. Without Mama asking me, I told her from the bottom of my heart, "I love you, Mama, I really do."

After a long time of listening, Mama asked me to leave so that she could sleep. I left and went into the living room to watch television with George. Later, I went in to check on her, and at first she seemed fine. She seemed to be resting, yet something seemed to be wrong. My first instinct was to not wake Mama up for fear that she would be mad at me. But something else told me to walk closer to the bed. I tiptoed closer and found a bottle of pills half empty laying on their side on the night stand. I knew right away what Mama had done. I ran to George and told him what I saw. George tried to get Mama up but she wouldn't come around. I thought she might be dead. Her body was limp. George said we didn't have much time and ran to the phone. He called for an ambulance. While we waited, George made me stay with Mama as he tried to locate Daddy. When he couldn't find him, he called Aunt Marilyn and asked her to come over and stay with me while he went to the hospital with Mama. When the ambulance arrived, they took Mama out on a stretcher and I cried out, "Please don't die Mama, Please don't die!"

I waited in the house alone, crying, until Aunt Marilyn arrived and stayed with me.

When Mama finally came home from the hospital, nothing was said about her attempt at suicide. Us kids tried to be kind and compassionate to her. Daddy stayed away as much as possible.

Light Beyond the Darkness

41
Broken Arm   June, 1975

It was Summer at last. No school and time to play
<u>all</u> day. One bright summer day Mama and Daddy both
had to work. Butch and George didn't have to work until
the afternoon so they were at home with me during the
morning. Eddie was there too. It seemed as though the
boys always had a friend or cousin over. George and
Eddie decided to take a short cruise in George's red
Challenger. Butch made George and Eddie take me with
them. I loved riding in the back of George's sports car. It
was fast and very loud. He would turn the radio up full
blast in order to hear it over the dual exhaust system that
he had installed. George had gotten warnings and tickets
about his car being too loud, but he wouldn't change it
because it was cool to have a loud car. The joy ride never
lasted long enough for me.

Early that afternoon, both Butch and George had
to go to work at Wynn Dixie®. Butch seemed to be a
little irritated about something. Maybe it was because
our parents said I could stay home alone. His girlfriend,
Robin, (she lived in the house right behind us) was over
and she said that she would stay with me or that I could
go to her house until our parents were home. Butch
thought that I was much too young to stay by myself.

Robin and I were in the bathroom, she was
showing me how to put on lipstick as Butch and George
were getting dressed for work. Just as George was
putting on his tie, Butch came in to the bathroom and
asked to borrow Robin's lipstick for a minute. Right when
George was ready to walk out the door, Butch put a dab of
lipstick on his cheek as a joke. George didn't think it was

very funny. George was actually very mad. I felt sorry for him and for some reason it reminded me of what Mama and I did to Daddy. I went into Mama's room and got another tube of lipstick and when Butch bent down, I rubbed it on his back of his shoulder. I laughed because now Butch had the tables turned on him. However, Butch didn't laugh at all. He didn't think my idea of revenge was very funny at all, and he chased me to my room where I slammed the door shut. I stood against the door trying to hold it shut so that Butch couldn't get it open. As he took a few steps back Butch told me that I was gonna get it, but I never knew how bad until he slammed against the door and busted it down. I flew across the room and hit the opposite wall with my left arm. I landed in a pile of stuffed animals and knew right away that I was hurt. Butch practically fell into the room and ran over to me. He was still angry and didn't realize that I was injured. He grabbed my left wrist which was swollen and purple and yanked me up to my feet. I screamed as I felt my elbow come out of the socket.

"Butch!" I screamed, "My arm, my arm, OWWWW!" I yelled, trying to tell him that I was hurt. George hadn't left yet and came running into the room. He took one look at my arm that was three times its normal size and he took a swing at Butch. When George saw my arm it must have been the last straw, because he drove for Butch and started pounding on him. Butch wasn't someone to take a swing at, he was strong and could beat up also everyone I knew. So Eddie jumped into the fight to help George. Eddie was even bigger than Butch and instead of fighting, he tried to separate Butch and George. However, he and Butch got involved in a fight. Crying from fear and pain, I stood with Robin and watched the three fighting. They fought for long time before Robin finally yelled out, "I think Cheri really needs to go to the hospital!"

Butch and George took me to the emergency room but the staff there wouldn't help me unless they had a parent's consent. Mama and Daddy should have been home from work by now. But they weren't at home. So I sat in the emergency waiting room for two hours while my brothers coached the nurses on what bars to call to reach our parents. They couldn't find them anywhere. Finally, a doctor was contacted about my situation. He looked at my completely purple arm and took the liberty to sign a release form to help me.

The x-ray showed that I had two broken bones and my elbow was out of the socket. I had to have a cast for six weeks. The worst part was when my parents finally came home; Daddy was furious. He and Butch had been in many arguments in the past and Butch was warned about his bad temper. Butch had punched several holes in the walls when he was either fighting with George or was mad at Mama. Butch and George fought as often as Mama and Daddy did. Their fights always included punching, blood and on occasion weapons such as large wrenches or crutches. When the boys fought, I'd hide in my room and prayed that God would save them from killing each other.

Daddy made Butch pack his clothes and move out of the house for breaking my arm. It was all my fault that he had to leave. I felt like I caused everyone to be miserable. Because I felt so guilty, it was difficult to talk to Butch for a long time after that. One month after he left, he joined the Army® and moved out of state. I never really knew how to say, "I'm sorry," but wrote to each other and became very close while he was away.

Light Beyond the Darkness

42

Mama's Boyfriend Horace   November, 1975

Mama met a new man. He was from Germany and his name was Horace. He was a big man with red curly hair. I didn't get to know him very well because Mama said that he was married. Every time we went to Horace's house I had to wait in the car while Mama went inside. Sometimes, I just laid back and took a nap in the car. Usually, Horace would walk Mama out to the car when it was time to go and he would talk to me then. He had a German accent.

There came the day when Mama got mad at Horace. She eventually got mad at all her boyfriends, and ended the relationships on bad terms. I figured that Mama either embarrassed her boyfriends, scared them away by yelling, or tried to kill them. One day, Mama was angry at Horace and we stopped by his house. I waited outside as usual. I don't know what Mama did inside that house but when she came running out, she jumped in the car and said, "I guess I showed him." We never saw Horace again after that.

43
Adventures On Our Boat   May, 1976

I loved to fish but our little flat-bottom eleven-foot boat wasn't made for deep salt water fishing. However, Daddy and George got much use out of it. They would get up early and take the boat to the Manatee River and little creeks that were close by our house. They would put the boat in the water at the boat dock that Mama took me to a few years before. Every time we went to the dock I would remember that day with Mama, and as soon as the thought came to my mind, I would quickly try to think of something else. I would try to think of fishing or Baby swimming in the water. I wanted to think of something good because I still felt so guilty for telling Mama that I loved her more than Daddy. I just wanted to forget that day.

Daddy liked to cast net for mullet. He and George had taken me with them a few times when they went cast nettin' from shore. There was lots of good fishing around the Manatee River and it was a lot of fun for me even though I didn't get to fish.

One day, Daddy came home with a great surprise. It was an eighteen-foot boat. It was big enough to take into the Gulf of Mexico. He said that we could go fishing on Sundays.

Every Sunday, George, Mama, Daddy and I would get up early and go out fishing on the boat. When Butch was at home on leave he would go with us, but he didn't like fishing very much. We would stay out all day. Often we'd stay out on the boat so long that we'd get caught in the afternoon rain shower. Sometimes, the showers were light showers and other times they were very scary storms. We had lots of adventures out on our boat.

We caught great fish during our excursions into the Gulf of Mexico and even in the Manatee River. We caught several sharks and Daddy once caught a huge stingray. That stingray was so big that it dragged our boat across the mouth of the river. It took Daddy almost forty-five minutes to bring it in and Daddy's hand had blisters from the reel. The fight was so intense that the tip of Daddy's pole broke off during the struggle. The stingray was too big to bring into the boat, so Daddy tied his line onto the side of the boat and slowly drove the boat back to the dock. Usually we let stingrays go, but Daddy said this one was big enough to make scallops out of. As we pulled into the dock the hook broke in half and we could see the stingray as he slowly swam away in the shallow waters. It was one of the most exciting days out on the boat.

44
To Catch a Shark   June, 1976

There were many fond memories from our weekly fishing trips. It was always exciting to catch a shark. I had only caught the small spoon sharks. Everyone else, however, had caught up sharks while out fishing in the Manatee River or Tampa Bay. One late afternoon, when Daddy brought in about a three-foot shark, I asked him if I could have the jaws. I didn't expect Daddy to pull out his knife and cut out the jaws right then and there. But he had already had quite a few beers and must have felt brave. He cut out the jaws as blood squirted out and began to cover the back of the boat. After completing the difficult task, Daddy reached over to me with the toothless shark and pretended to attack me. As it thrashed around, blood continued to spill from its tangled toothless jaws, I felt sorry. Sorry that I had asked for the jaws in the first place. Daddy put the shark back in the water; it swam for a few feet, then it stopped and started to sink down into the water. I did save the jaws. But to me they didn't seem to be the trophy that I had imagined they would be. To me, they were a cruel reminder of something I had destroyed.

45
Truth or Dare

My first boyfriend. We met through the phone. Tommie Lee and I were playing Truth or Dare. It was one of our favorite games. I took a double dare from Tommie Lee to call a boy named John and talk to him. He was the cousin of a friend our Tommie Lee's. I had never seen him nor did I know anything about him, but it was a dare and so I called him. We spoke on the phone for an hour. After that day, John and I became very good friends. He was four years older than me. We spoke to each other every day and sometimes our conversations lasted four to five hours. With George working, Butch away in the army, and Mama and Daddy out all the time, I stayed home alone a lot. When I was home alone and became frightened, I would call John. He had a way of calming my nerves and making me feel better. Even though John lived in Palmetto, I felt like he was always there for me. I felt like I was falling in love.

At eleven years old, I felt as though this young man loved me more than anyone. It seemed as though he really cared for me. And though we had never met in person, no one had shown me as much attention as John and I adored him. My parents only knew him by phone but liked him because he was very polite. One day, John decided it was time that we met and he wanted to ride his bike all the way over to my house. Strict instructions were given to me each time my parents left me home alone. First, no one was allowed in the house and second, I wasn't allowed to go outside the yard. So, I met John in the street in front of my house and we talked as he sat on his bike. He didn't look anything like I had imagined. I thought he would be tall, dark and handsome. Instead, he was medium height, and skinny as a rail. His hair was blond and frizzy. His appearance didn't attract me at first, but I knew how much he cared about me so I liked him regardless of what he looked like.

46
Mama's New Car

Grandma California would sometimes pick me up at school. I would then go to Grandma's and spend the afternoon until Mama picked me up after work. Mama was still working at the hospital part-time as a L.P.N. One day, Mama called Grandma and asked her to bring me home because something had happened to the car. Grandma quickly got all of my things together and we rushed over to see what was wrong. We were anxious to see if Mama had gotten into another accident. As we pulled into our driveway we were extremely surprised! Our brown, four-door Buick was gone. In our driveway was a brand new, two-door, blue and white Mustang. It was small and sporty!

Grandma and I ran into the house as Mama stepped proudly out of her room, beaming with pride. "Did you see my new car?" she asked. I jumped up and down with excitement, "You mean that's <u>our</u> car?" Mama proudly told us that it was her own car, and she had financed it herself. Now that she had a job she could be independent. She was extremely proud of herself, and I was proud of her too. She asked Grandma to come drive over so that she could go with us to pick up the Buick back at the car dealer.

Grandma was worried. "What did Lo think about you getting a car of your own?" She asked in a concerned old-fashioned tone. Mama exclaimed that Daddy didn't know yet, and that she was going to tell him when he got home from work. The first words out of Grandma's mouth were "Lo's gonna kill you."

There was a fight, but Mama got to keep her car. I was glad. I was proud of that car and proud of Mama for getting it herself.

47

Why Did I Do That?   September, 1976

It was one of those days that Daddy didn't come home and Mama left in a fury to catch Daddy at the bar with another woman. As her car was leaving the driveway, I was dialing the number to my knight in shining armor, John. I, like Mama liked the attention that John gave me and I learned quickly what to say on the phone when I called him. I was already upset and lonely. I told him how I was scared that Mama wouldn't find Daddy and that she would come home and take it out on me. I cried over the phone.

It wasn't long before he suggested that he come over. I wanted attention but I never expected him to suggest that he break the rules and come over. At first, I said, "No, the rules are no one is allowed in while my parents are away." John said that he would park his bike in the back and that my parents would never know he was there. Though I was scared, I also wanted to see John and an hour later he was at my house. We were alone for the first time.

We talked a little while and then we kissed. He asked me if I wanted to make love and I really had no idea what he meant. He said that it was what two people did when they were in love. I said, "Okay," after all, John and I were in love. I had no idea what I had just gotten myself into. Later, I asked John, terrified of what had just happened, "Why? Why did you do this to me?"
John replied, "You wanted to."

Daddy and Mama pulled up into the driveway in Daddy's car. John made a quick dash to the back door, jumped on his bike and pedaled away. I ran into the bathroom and cried. Mama and Daddy were in their own world and didn't notice that I was upset. I felt so bad. What was I going to tell my parents? I was so scared. If they knew they would kill me. So many thoughts and emotions were running through me. I felt guilty. I knew what I had done was wrong. I hated John and wanted to blame it all on him. I never wanted to talk to him again. That night John called me and this time <u>he</u> was crying. He felt so bad about what happened earlier. He felt terrible for hurting me. He promised that he would never do anything like that again and that from that point on, he would obey the rules. I never felt the same for him after that. I was angry at myself and at him. My whole life changed after that one day.

> *I Thessalonians 4:3 (NIV)*
> *It is God's will that you should avoid sexual immorality.*

48
"Help Me! She Shot Me!"

It all began when Daddy didn't come home from work. Mama got mad and decided to go and search the bars. We finally found Daddy's car at the Blue Dolphin Inn, it was a bar in Bradenton. She went inside while I waited out in the car. I assumed it would take a while; just like all the other times before. I had just laid down on the front seat when Mama came charging back out to the car. Mama jumped in and started cussing about Daddy. She told me that Daddy was flirting with some red-headed woman in the bar. Before starting the car and driving away, Mama waited to see if Daddy was coming outside. Daddy never walked out the door. Mama was fumin' mad and decided that she had had enough. Before driving away, Mama drove up next to Daddy's car. She reached in her purse and pulled out a knife. My first thought was, "Oh no, not again." Mama jumped out of the car and began jamming the knife into each of Daddy's tires. Although, I knew that wasn't very nice, I was relieved to see Mama using the knife on Daddy's tires and not Daddy.

Mama decided to stop at Ray's on the way home even though it was out of the way. She wanted to have "a beer or two." I sat there quietly listening as Mama gathered a sympathetic ear from the men and women at our table. She told them how Daddy ran around on her and how bad he had hurt her. She told them that Daddy went to the bar all the time and was never home to raise us kids. She made him out to be a terrible husband and father. As I listened I felt sorry for Daddy. Although he did do some or most of the things that Mama said, she had done everything she accused Daddy of doing, too. He was definitely stopping at the bar after work, yet Mama went to the bar all the time too. Why was she all upset? I didn't think she was being fair at all.

At first, Mama's story started out with tears and a cry of sympathy, but the more she talked about it and the more she drank, the angrier she became. She began to joke about "killing the son-of-bit-h." Her friends all laughed and joked that Mama wouldn't hurt a fly. I sat there silently and cringed inside. They didn't know Mama. I sat back listening to everyone tell Mama how sweet and wonderful she was and that she deserved better. I sat there thinking to myself, "They just don't know her. She has them all fooled." Mama was good at fooling people and she always put on a good first impression. She could be sweet, innocent and very well-mannered. But, the other side of Mama scared me to death. She would rage with jealously, envy and bitterness over many different people and many different things. Very few people knew this side of Mama. Most of our relatives had seen it a time or two, but neighbors and friends would never believed me when I told them that my Mama wasn't always so sweet and loving. To them, Mama was the nicest mom on the block.

Returning home from the bar we found Eddie, George and his friend Darrell at the house. The boys gathered around Mama as she cried and told the story once again of finding Daddy with another woman at the bar. As Mama sat there and talked to the boys about Daddy, I felt very thankful that George, my cousin Eddie and Darrell were at home when we arrived. I had been alone with Mama too many times when situations like this arose and it wasn't easy for me, nor was it pleasant.

Mama didn't get the response she desired from Eddie and George about Daddy being with another woman. Mama *accused* Daddy of "running around" all the time. Everywhere Daddy went Mama *thought* that he was out meeting women. She even accused him of dating other women when he and George were out fishing. She said he probably found a woman for George too and therefore George would tattle on Daddy. I always thought that was funny because George never had a girlfriend. George told Mama that he and Daddy didn't do anything but fish, but Mama never believed him. Now that Mama wanted George to believe her, he wouldn't. George thought that Mama was exaggerating or just accusing Daddy again like she had done so many times in the past. Eddie really admired my Daddy and wouldn't say anything negative against him. Darrell was just to quiet to take any sides.

Mama went into the her bedroom and upon returning into the Florida room she had Daddy's double-barrel shotgun under her arm, two bullets in one hand and a beer in the other. She opened the beer and sat down, "This should take care of the bastard." Now Mama had Eddie and Darrell's attention. Eddie said, "Aunt Carolyn, you can't go and kill Uncle Lo." George still didn't take her seriously. Knowing what Mama could do, I never doubted her for a minute.

As the night grew on, Darrell and Eddie left. George headed off to bed and Mama made me sleep in her room. For some reason whenever Daddy didn't come home, I always had to sleep in Mama's room. I hated sleeping in her room because she and Daddy always fought when he finally did get home. I knew that it was going to be another sleepless night.

Mama carried the double-barrel shotgun into her bedroom and laid it on the bed. Upon entering the room, she gave me directions to help her push a heavy wooden dresser in front of the door. She didn't want Daddy coming into their bedroom when he got home. The dresser was stocked full of clothes, plus had a large mirror on top. It was heavy, but inch by inch we pushed it the few feet to make it sit directly in front of the only door to the bedroom.

The loaded gun made me feel uneasy. As Mama laid down on the bed she picked up the gun and laid it next to the bed on the floor. She instructed me to lay next to her. The curtains were drawn shut across the windows. The room was dimly lit by a small night light in the bathroom. Silently, I took deep breaths trying to calm myself and so not to upset Mama. I prayed silently to God that I would sleep in peace. I prayed for my own safety and for Daddy's. I prayed that the night would end quickly and that tomorrow would be a better day. I continued to pray until I drifted off to sleep.

Bang! Bang!

"Let me in this room, Carol!" Daddy said in anger as he pounded on the door. Startled, I quickly sat up in bed. I had never even heard Daddy come home. I looked at the alarm clock that sat high upon Daddy's dresser. It read 3:30 a.m.

Mama woke up quickly and was yelling back at Daddy.

"Where the hell have you been? F---ing your new girlfriend? Go back and sleep at her house." Mama yelled at Daddy.

"Where do you think I've been?" Daddy replied, "Someone sliced my tires! I had to walk all the way home! Now I'm tired and I want a blanket and my alarm clock!"

Immediately, I jumped out of bed and headed towards Daddy's dresser to get his alarm clock. Mama rolled out of bed, grabbed the shotgun and told me to stop. "He's not getting a damn thing outta here."

"Carol, you know I have to work in the morning. I mean it, I want my alarm clock and the blanket!" Even though Daddy's speech was slurred I could tell he was extremely angry at Mama. It sounded as though he knew she was the one that had sliced his tires.

"Lo, you are a lying son-of-a-bi--h! I know you went to that red-head's house and when she saw how

176

little your peck-- was, she kicked you out. Isn't that it, Lo?" Mama stood with the shotgun pointed at the closed door. I was in shock. I stood next to Mama, staring at the gun.
I whispered, "Mama don't shoot. Please, don't do it."
I was rubbing my hands together nervously, only stopping for a moment to wipe my tears on my sleeve. Part of me was too scared to even stand next to Mama. I was scared she may change her mind and accidentally (or not) shoot me! Yet, I didn't want to just stand by and watch Daddy get killed. Daddy didn't even know that Mama had a gun! What was I supposed to do? "Oh God, please help me?!" I prayed to myself.

Mama ignored me as Daddy started banging harder on the door. "Let me in my DAMN room!" I knew Daddy was extremely mad because he rarely cussed. He was banging and shoving and trying to force the door open. The dresser began to budge and I screamed out, "No, Daddy don't do it! Don't come in!" I didn't want to see Daddy killed. I was scared to death. Hyperventilating, I cried out, "No! No! No!" I didn't want to see Daddy hurt, I didn't want this to really be happening! I thought to myself that I would rather be dead than to live in this nightmare!

In a calm voice, Mama looked at the door and looked back at me, "Go lay down on the bed and go to sleep Cheri."
Daddy continued to rush the door trying desperately to knock it down.
"But, Mama...." I cried.
"Cheri, don't make me tell you again. Go lay down, and go to sleep." she said sternly.
Sobbing, I ran over to the bed. I threw myself down and covered my head with pillows. I didn't want to hear Daddy's scream. I didn't want to hear my Daddy die. I didn't want to hear Mama kill Daddy. Hysterically, I started praying, "Please dear God, Please dear God! Please,

help my Daddy! Please dear God, please don't let Mama shoot him! Please dear God..."

BOOM!

There was silence. I lay there just for a second and then I rolled over... "Oh no! No, God, Please, no!" I jumped out of the bed to hear Daddy screaming in the dining room, "MY GOD, SHE SHOT ME! HELP ME, SHE SHOT ME!"

I rushed over to the dresser that blocked the door. Daddy was moaning on the other side. Hysterically, I cried out to him, "DADDY!" I didn't want him to die. I wanted to run to him, but I couldn't. I was stuck in the room with Mama. I tried to push the dresser away from the door but it wouldn't move. I cried, jumping up and down, pleading with Mama to help me move the dresser that now displayed a cantaloupe size hole in the top back portion where the bullet had busted through.

"Calm down Cheri. I didn't kill him. If I wanted to kill him, I would've used both bullets and I would've aimed much higher." Mama stated matter of factly.

Her words didn't soothe my aching heart. All I could think of was Daddy bleeding to death in the next room. Mama seemed to be indifferent to everything that just happened. I was still attempting to move the dresser. I ran around it, pulling, tugging, and begging Mama to help me. George ran in to the dining room, "What the hell happened?" He asked. Daddy answered him as if in amazement, "She shot me!" "Daddy!" I cried out in agony.

Inside the room, Mama turned to me and told me to go lay down and get some sleep. How could I lie down and sleep when Daddy was shot? I wanted to tell Daddy that I loved him. I wanted to tell him how much I really truly loved him, but I was too afraid of Mama. Who still had the gun in her hands. I thought of the day she tried to make me jump off the bridge. What would she do if I told Daddy I loved him? Would she shoot me? Would she make me tell Daddy, as he lay there dying, that I loved her more than him? Daddy was moaning and Mama turned to me and shouted "Get in bed and go to sleep!"

I ran to the bed and threw myself down and within seconds, I passed out and didn't wake up until the sheriff started banging on the bedroom window. When I first awoke, I thought it was all a dream, a terrible dream. Then I sat up in bed and saw the dresser, the door and the holes and then the sheriff hit the window again. With my heart pounding out of my chest, I jumped out of bed, fell to my knees and lay there crying. I was living in a nightmare.

The sheriff said that Daddy was in the hospital, and that his condition was serious but not critical. At the hospital, Daddy had lied and told the police that he was shot while out shark fishing. (It was custom to shoot large sharks before bringing them onto the boat.) Daddy had told George, on the way to the hospital, what he planned to tell the police the shark fishing lie and Daddy wanted George to lie too. Daddy told the police that George and he were out on the boat and when George shot the gun it ricocheted off the aluminum boat and hit him. George was nervous and the sheriff could tell that the story was a cover up. The sheriff convinced George that Daddy confessed the truth (this was a trick on the sheriff's behalf to find out what really happened). George replied, "The real truth?" When the sheriff nodded, George told the sheriff about Mama, the shotgun and me being trapped in her room. The sheriff came to our house immediately. No charges were ever pressed.

49
I Wanted To Forget It All

It was a school day and I rode the bus to school like normal. I attended Sugg Middle School. Mama had said that I could stay home from school, and even though I was really tired, I was too scared to stay at home. I kept thinking to myself that it was all a nightmare. I wanted to wake up and forget about the whole big mess. Deep inside I asked myself, "What should I have done to stop Mama?" I felt tortured that somehow I didn't do enough to prevent Mama from shooting Daddy. I decided to pretend as though it was a dream. But as the day went on it got harder and harder for me to hold everything in. All day, I fought back tears. My two good friends, Kathy and Jennifer, noticed that something was wrong. They asked me and I just shrugged my shoulders and walked away. Though I tried to hide my anguish I couldn't fake a smile. Kathy and Jennifer thought that maybe I had a problem with a boy. They figured I liked someone and he liked someone else. How could I tell them that last night, or rather, this morning, my mother shot my father? Class after class, I relived the moment that I thought Daddy was dying outside the door. I wondered over and over what I could have done differently to stop Mama.

The last class of the day was Chemistry with Mr. White. In one way I felt relieved that school was almost over and I didn't have to walk through the motions and hide my emotions . Yet, did I really want to go home? Suddenly, I felt so overwhelmed I thought I was going to explode. I wanted to scream, no cry, no I wanted to die; I just didn't want to face what happened last night! I didn't want to go home and I didn't want to be at school. I felt alone. No one cared or understood anything about me. The tears started to swell and I closed my eyes and rocked back and forth in my chair, trying to calm myself down.

My teacher looked at me. Immediately he noticed that something was wrong. Mr. White was a good teacher and I suppose he suspected that things weren't perfect at home for me. He seemed to sense that I wasn't like other kids who attended my upper class school and he tried to get me to open up to him. This time when he asked what was wrong, though I tried to continue to hide my true feelings, with tears softly flowing, and I whispered, "Nothing." Mr. White sent me back to his office. He then went to another classroom where Kathy also had chemistry and asked her teacher if she could come in and talk with me. There, I opened up to Kathy and told her of my horrifying experience the previous night. She persuaded me to tell Mr. White and he sat quietly listening and sympathizing. Mr. White encouraged me to tell the school counselor and said that they could get help for my parents. I told him that I would think about it. I felt so overwhelmed, all I really wanted to do was die. I didn't want help. I didn't want counseling, it was too late. In so many ways I felt that I had dug my own grave. I wanted to get out of the dark and dreary nightmare that seemed to go on, day after day. I wanted out of the fighting, drinking, cussing, and lying. And it wasn't just Mama and Daddy's lies that bothered me now. No one liked me at school; no one really cared and I knew why. In an attempt to be cool and fit in I, myself, had told so many lies. Who would ever believe me about my parents? Even Kathy and Jennifer talked behind my back. Mr. White was the only one who believed me.

I don't remember much of the rest of that day. I rode the bus home and I can't remember who was there or what happened. All I know is that I couldn't handle any more pain. I wanted to forget and some of it I did.

Light Beyond the Darkness

50
Never Tell Family Secrets

Mr. White continued to ask me if I had spoken to my school counselor. I hadn't spoken to them at the time. But one day in late October when I was feeling low, I decided to skip a class. When I got back to school I was called into the counselor's office. She asked me why I had skipped and I told her the truth. I wanted to escape. I told her how I thought about running away from home again, but yet, somehow I knew that wouldn't solve any of the problems I had at home. I skipped class to just get away from everything and think about what I should do. Then I went on to tell her about my home life. I didn't tell her everything. I didn't want to make it sound too bad. it sure felt good to get some of it off my chest. It felt good to tell someone how *I* felt.

After school that afternoon, I walked up the driveway feeling a little relieved. After telling the counselor about my home life she forgot all about the class I skipped. If Mama found out that I had skipped a class she would kill me. So I felt as though I had gotten myself out of trouble. "How clever of me," I thought to myself and I smiled. However, as I walked in the front door, my smile quickly disappeared when I saw Mama's angry face. Had the counselor remembered after all and called Mama to tell her what I had done?

SLAP! Before I could even say hello, the palm of her hand slapped hard against my left cheek. "What was that for?" I asked, rubbing my cheek, trying to act innocent.
"Who did you talk to today?" Mama asked accusingly.

I thought for sure she was mad about the class that I had skipped and her question threw me off. Confused, I answered, "Nobody." Then immediately after the word came out of my mouth I remembered *what* I had told the counselor. I had spoken to the counselor about Mama and how I hated living in all the drinking and fighting. Oh, no. This can't be happening to me. How could Mama find out about my conversation with a counselor at school?

"Tell me who you talked to today!" Mama demanded as she grabbed my shirt and dragged me over to the living room couch. With her eyes squinted and her mouth in an angry frown, she told me that the child welfare people went to the house while I was still at school. They received an anonymous call that I was being abused. Mama wanted to know where they would get such an idea. I continued to plead my innocence, knowing deep inside that I was lying to Mama, but too afraid to confront her with the truth. The more I lied, the madder she got. I knew she wasn't gonna believe me but I wasn't about to confess and tell her the truth. Mama scared me.

As I sat there on the couch, feeling as though I was being interrogated, Mama told me that abused children are taken away from their homes. They live in orphanages. They have no toys, no animals, and they never see their family again. Mama gave me an ultimatum; either I tell the child welfare people that I was lying and made up everything about the abuse, or she would let them take me away to the orphanage. Mama scared me, but the loneliness of living in an orphanage scared me more.

The weeks that followed were terrible for me. The only time Mama and Daddy spoke to me was to coach me on what to say to the new child welfare counselor. Mama would ask me questions that she thought the counselor might ask. I answered, "I don't know," to almost all of them. Mama sternly prompted me on the right way to answer them. Sometimes, Mama would make me say the answers over and over again, until it sounded like I really meant what I was saying. She threatened that if I didn't try harder to convince the counselor of how happy I was, then I would be taken away. I would never see her, Daddy, Butch or George again.

When it finally came time to meet with the counselor, it was difficult to lie to her. I think I wanted the truth to be known. I wanted my life to be over, yet, I didn't like the ultimatum. After leaving the counselor's office, I felt angry that she, a professional didn't see the truth through the lies in my testimony. I wanted help, but now, I knew that <u>no one</u> could help me. I was alone. No one knew me; no one cared. I felt as though I lived in a glass bubble. I could see everyone around me but they couldn't see the real me. No one tried to reach in to my glass world, so fragile and weak, and pull me out. I figured that if I banged on the glass to ask for help, they'd all just look at me and wonder, "What's wrong with her?" No one wanted to help me. No one cared. I might as well die, no one would even notice.

Going to bed each night, I prayed for God to let me die a quiet death in my sleep. As I prayed that God would let me die, I wondered to myself if God was even listening. Maybe He had given up on me too.

Looking back, I didn't know it then but God was there with me. I know now that He held me, He cared for me, and He stood with me in my glass bubble. He had plans for me and He was there helping me cope day by day, hour by hour, minute by minute.

Psalm 139:1-12,17,18.(TLB)

O Lord, You have examined my heart and know everything about me. You know when I sit or stand. When

*far away you know my every thought.
You chart the path ahead of me, and
tell me where to stop and rest. Every
moment, you know where I am. You
know what I am going to say before I
even say it. You both precede and
follow me, and place your hand of
blessing on my head. ... How precious it
is Lord, to realize that you are thinking
about me constantly! I can't even count
how may times a day your thoughts
turn towards me. And when I waken
in the morning, you are still thinking of
me!*

51
Through the Darkness, God Was There
November, 1976

Most of my time was now spent alone; Butch was in the Army, George was usually gone, Daddy stilled worked two jobs and Mama worked full-time too. I found things to occupy my time. I took long walks with Baby. Sometimes, I would find secret little secluded areas by a creek or in the woods. I would stay there and daydream about what life could have been like. There were so many different emotions going through my growing body. I felt deserted, unloved, alone...I felt desperate. Sometimes, when Mama and Daddy were gone, I felt angry. I wanted someone at home with me. I wanted someone to care about me. I wanted someone to show me love and attention like the other kids my age. Since my family had seemed to have forgotten about me, I decided to look for love and attention else where.

Eric was a boy at school. He was in my grade and his father worked with Daddy. Eric had the reputation of a "trouble-maker." Since neither of us were actually allowed to date, our relationship existed primarily at school. We considered ourselves boyfriend and girlfriend. We wrote notes and spoke to each other between classes. We went out for about six months when one day Eric broke up with me. I was hurt and that night when Mama and Daddy decided to go out to the bar, I felt even more hurt.

Between Eric, my feelings of loneliness, and the dreadful thought of Mama and Daddy coming home in

189

another fight, I decided I had had enough. I decided to run away. I packed a couple of things in a large purse and headed out on foot to the beach. Eric lived on the beach and of course I wanted him to find me and tell me that he had made a mistake. I wanted him to say, "I love you, Cheri and I always will."

The beach was nine miles west of my home and as I walked through the back streets and along the highway, I did my usual thing; I daydreamed. What if Eric saw me but didn't care that I had run away? I couldn't handle that rejection. What if Mama and Daddy drove by? They would kill me. Where would I stay once I got out to the beach? I had no idea. I was confused, and for an instant I thought about turning back and going home. Yet, I knew it was too late to turn back. If Mama and Daddy got home before I did, then they would be furious with me for leaving the house. I would be in a tremendous amount of trouble. It was definitely too late to turn back.

I was frightened as the afternoon turned into evening. Yet, through the darkness, and the agony, I realize that God was with me on my journey. I didn't trust in Him then as I do now, but that didn't take His hand of protection away from me. His hand definitely blessed me with protection as I walked that long and dangerous journey.

One of the scariest parts of the journey was when a man pulled over and tried to get me to ride with him. I said, "No thank you," several times but he would not leave me alone. He continued to drive slowly on the shoulder of the highway next to me and ask questions. He tried to coax me into his car. Scared of what might happened I prayed for God to help me. I feared that he would force me into his car. Faithful as God is, He sent a police officer by. As the policeman slowed down the man pulled away. The policeman stopped and asked if I was okay. He asked me where I was headed and I lied and told him I was headed home. I told him that I lived on the

Light Beyond the Darkness

beach. He, too, offered to give me a ride but I insisted on walking. He had no idea that I was a runaway and let me walk away.

As the sky grew from dusk to darkness, I decided to ask for God's help even though I wasn't sure that He still cared about me. Looking to the sky, I prayed, "Please, watch out for me. Please, help me."

The moon that night was like no other I had ever seen. On a small road with no lights, the moon shone brightly like a giant glowing ball as I walked towards my destination. It lit my path and gave me peace. It was the largest moon I had ever seen. (And still to this day, I have never witnessed a moon as bright as the one in the sky that night.) Since the night that Mama left me at Linger Lodge®, I was especially afraid of the dark. I even went to bed with my light on. Now, here I was alone, in the night, in the darkness. I had no one else to turn to but God and He lit the moon so bright that I could see the road in front of me. He lit my path so that I could feel safe. He carried me out of the darkness.

When I arrived at Manatee beach, I walked another couple of miles along the water until I reached the beach directly across from Eric's house. Separating the highway and parking lot from the beach was a pile of large rocks. Amongst those rocks, I found a space that sheltered me on three sides and blocked some of the chilly winter air. The only opening faced the waves as they crashed against the soft sandy shore. Curled up in the sand with a rock as my pillow, I heard the cars as they sped by. I was frightened. I wanted the safety of my room. I wanted to be in my own bed with a soft pillow. I knew then that even though things were bad at home; it would be worse not to have a home at all. I cried. I knew that I had made a terrible mistake. I prayed to God again to keep me safe. As I fell asleep the noise of traffic drifted and the soft soothing sound of the ocean grew sweetly in my ears. The rolling sound of the water lifted my worries and carried me into pleasant dreams.

> *Psalm 139: 6-12 (TLB)*
>
> *This is too glorious, too wonderful to believe! I can never be lost to your spirit! I can never get away from my God! If I go up to heaven, you are there; if I go down to the place of the dead, you are there. If I ride the morning winds to the farthest oceans, even there your hand will guide me, your strength will support me. If I try to hide in the darkness, the night becomes light around me. For even darkness cannot hide from God; to you the night shines as bright as day. Darkness and light are both alike to you.*

The next morning, I walked to the Seven-Eleven® and called home. I still wanted to go home even though I was afraid that Mama and Daddy would beat me. When I called Mama answered the phone and when she heard my voice she started to cry. She came and picked me up and I told her all about the previous night.

Mama accepted me without any conditions. For some odd reason, she didn't even act mad. Daddy, on the other hand, was furious and wanted to whip me, but Mama protected me from his spanking. When Mama asked me why I ran away, and all I could say was, "I don't know." She didn't press any further but left me alone.

52
Just To Be Cool

Eleven was a hard age for me. It had been awhile since Mama and Daddy had any big blow out fights but life was still hard for me. All the decisions I had to make seemed to make life very difficult. I wanted to be cool, and I wanted boys to like me. I wanted friends. It was time for me to choose right from wrong. It was the time that I needed God's guidance, yet that was exactly what I didn't want. I knew in my heart what God would choose and that wasn't what it took to be cool or liked, so I decided that I could handle issues with right or wrong, with popularity, and with boys, all by myself. God didn't matter much to me now. I wanted approval so desperately I was willing to take a few risks.

Was it love that I was looking for or just simply attention? I didn't know then and I didn't want to stop to figure it out. Looking back, I know that I had the most powerful love of all in my heart; the love of Jesus. Yet, I didn't stop to acknowledge Him. God was the One who loved me the most; He cared for me and He was the only one who never left my side; not even when I was willing to run away from Him.

Colossians 1-21 (NIV)
Once you were alienated from God and were enemies in your minds because of your evil behavior. But now He has reconciled you by Christ's physical body through death to present you are

holy in his sight, without blemish and free from accusation.

53
Bad Choices   February, 1977

While riding the bus to and from school, I met up
with a gang of boys that lived in a housing development
called Harbor Hills.   Most of the guys had wealthy
families and they were used to getting what they wanted.
Tom, Bobby, Frances, Darrin, Greg, and B.J. were all
ranging from my age to high school. A couple of the boys
did some drugs and the rest of them drank a lot. I got
involved with them and soon had to make some very
serious choices. One thing led to another and it wasn't
long before I had made the wrong decision more than
once. I smoked marijuana, drank alcohol, and became
promiscuous. I got involved with one of the boys and
pretty soon we had overstepped our boundaries. It meant
nothing to the boy and only pain to me. It didn't take
long before the whole gang knew about our one-time
episode and that's when a different boy decided to take
advantage of me.
I was out on a walk, I decided to stop by one the
guys' house. He and his brother were the only two at
home. He had heard about what went on and asked if it
was true. I told him that it was true. I didn't act shy nor
did I act like I was ashamed of what had happened. Deep
inside, I was hurting very much, but I just wanted to be
cool, so I acted as though it was no big deal. The boy
hassled me for never doing anything like that with him. I
laughed and didn't say a word. He asked me to look at
something in his bedroom and I followed him in. In his
room, he flirted with me and for some reason I liked it. I
thought that maybe he had a crush on me. We began

what I thought was an innocent act of kissing, but as it progressed further, I was unable to stop him. I told him no several times and began to scream. Nothing helped. His little brother, who was my age, even came into the room but instead of helping me, stood there and watched. At my first opportunity, I ran out of the room and then out of the house and as far away as I could. I wanted to believe that it was all just another nightmare and that it never really happened.

> *Ephesians 5:3-4(NIV)*
> *But among you there must not be even a hint of sexual immorality or of any kind of impurity, or of greed, because these are improper for God's holy people. Nor should there be obscenity, foolish talk or coarse joking, which are out of place but rather thanksgiving.*

On the way home, I tried to kill myself by running in front of a car. The car swerved and my attempt at suicide failed. I went home and sat alone for hours. It was the first time that I was glad that no one was home. I couldn't stop crying and I didn't want to tell anyone what I had just been through. I knew that if I told Mama she would probably kill me. (Every time I got hurt, Mama said it was my own fault. Even once when a dog bit me in the leg.) I was too ashamed to explain everything to my brothers or to Daddy. There was no one to tell. And because I had forgotten all about God, I figured that God had turned His back on me. Why would He stick around when I didn't pray or obey His commandments.

Part of me felt as if I deserved being raped; after all, I had been promiscuous and I did enjoy kissing him. I sat alone in my room and shouted loudly to the ceiling, "What is wrong with me? Why do I do this?" I crumbled to the floor, curled up in a ball and cried in a soft whisper, "Why me God, Why me? I just want to die. Please just let me die."

I know now that what happened to me wasn't God's will. He wasn't punishing me or holding me accountable. Though I do believe that God is just, the terrifying actions of that young man were a result of Satan's presence in this world and a result of my poor decision- making. I no longer hold bitterness towards that young man, nor towards myself, for I know that my enemy doesn't lie in that boy but instead, in the rulers of darkness.

Ephesians 6:12
We wrestle not against flesh and blood, but
against principalities, against powers,
against the rulers of the darkness.

Light Beyond the Darkness

54
I Walked On Eggshells Day After Day

Deadly silence. It was as bad as the arguing. Mama and Daddy hardly spoke to one another. There was nothing but silence; no conversations, no dinners, no jokes, no boat trips. Silent barriers controlled our home. Tension was everywhere in the house. Softly I tiptoed around every spoken and unspoken word; afraid of what might be the outcome. It seemed as though I walked on eggshells day after day.

I asked God to stop my parents from fighting and now they hardly talk. What did I do? I hated the arguing and I hated the silence. Every day, I dreaded coming home from school. Mama was depressed. I heard rumors from relatives that Mama and Daddy were getting a divorce, but no one spoke to me. Now it wasn't just Mama that scared me, it was everything that scared me. I hated the silence and was afraid that just one word would send Mama off the deep end. I was afraid of the divorce. Yet, I didn't like the fighting and wanted it to stop. I was caught in the middle <u>again</u>. No longer did I ask why. I knew that I had made a lot of mistakes that God didn't approve of; I figured that I was being served my just punishment. It was punishment for losing my virginity, for trying drugs and for disobeying. I wondered how and if God could ever forgive me. I couldn't see a way. I knew that I couldn't kill myself. I thought that I would have to find a way to live through my situation on my own.

Romans 8: 37-39 (NIV)
In all these things we are more than conquerors through Him who loved us. For I am convinced that neither death, nor life, neither demons nor angels, neither the present, nor the future, nor any powers, neither height, nor depth, nor anything else in all creation will be able to separate us from the love of God that is in Christ Jesus our Lord.

Romans 8:1 (NIV)
Therefore, there is now no condemnation for those who are in Christ Jesus.

55
The Eggshells Cracked

The silence finally broke; the eggshells cracked and Mama finally exploded. She and I were the only ones home before I had to leave for school one day. I don't remember what I did, but I made Mama so angry she threatened to kill me. She told me that when I got home from school that day I would "really get it." I knew that she planned to beat me and she would never forget. That day was the longest day of my life. By the time school ended, I didn't know what to do.

During the bus ride home I confided in B.J. that Mama was mad at me and threatened to beat me when I got home. I told him that I was scared and didn't want to go home. He said that he would help. Instead of getting off the bus at my stop, I rode the bus into Harbor Hills and went to B.J.'s house. B.J. was a true friend and really stuck up for me when we were around the other guys in Harbor Hills. He told me about a fort that he had way out in the woods.

B.J. and I ate a snack at his house and then headed out to the fort. It was small but it would be a good hideout. The first night (it was a Friday), a few boys from Harbor Hills brought me a pair of jeans and a t-shirt and a bottle of brandy. We all got drunk. One of the boys stayed the night with me. I was so drunk that I couldn't even walk and stayed sick for two days after. By Monday, loneliness started to settle in. I wanted to talk to my Aunt Marilyn. I asked one of the guys to anonymously call her and tell her that I was okay. Tom said that he would canoe me over to Snead Island where Aunt Marilyn lived.

Snead Island was right across the Manatee River and didn't seem that far away. It didn't seem like that big of a deal to cross the Manatee River in a canoe. Every day I would ask him, "Can you please take me today?" Every day, he had a new reason why he couldn't take me across. Finally after almost a week of staying in the fort, I asked B.J. if I could go to his house when no one else was there to take a shower. He came to get me right after school and I took a shower at his house before anyone else came home. While I was there, I decided to call my Aunt.

Hearing her voice, I cried. Running away from Mama wasn't the right answer and I knew that now. I had gotten myself into more trouble and all I wanted was someplace safe to go. Aunt Marilyn said that she would come and get me and I could stay with her for a while.

I stayed at Aunt Marilyn's for a short time but it was such an inconvenience for everyone that I felt more out of place there than I did at home. My parents wouldn't let me transfer schools so someone had to drive me to and from school everyday. I could tell that I was just being a burden and after about a week, Tommie Lee and I were fighting like cats and dogs. One morning, Daddy picked me up to take me to school and suggested that I move back home with Mama. I decided he was right and I rode the bus home that afternoon.

56
Christmas Without Daddy   December, 1977

Mama took me with her to sign some papers. Daddy was going to meet her there. At the time, I had no idea what Mama and Daddy were doing. They had been separated for some time and I knew that they were thinking about a divorce, but I had no clue that it would come so soon. Instead of going into the office building with her, I sat and waited in the car. It seemed to take a long time, but I was used to waiting, sometimes hours, when Mama and Daddy went to the bar, so I amused myself until Mama returned.

When Mama returned from the office building she was crying. She cried all the way home. She told me that she and Daddy were divorced and that they were selling our house. I had to fight back the tears. I wondered if I would ever see Daddy again. I wondered where we would live. I wondered what would happen to me now.

Mama and Daddy had signed those papers just before Christmas. This would be my first Christmas without Daddy. I think Mama felt bad and so she bought me a lot of presents. I got a clock radio, blow dryer, and curling iron. I knew that the gifts were expensive and I appreciated Mama trying to make it a good Christmas for me. George had a very sweet girlfriend and she came over to spend Christmas with us. Her name was Caroline. She was so innocent and seemed to care a great deal for others. She and George gave me two of the most beautiful dresses I had ever seen. I opened the first one and almost started to cry. I had never had such an expensive dress before in my life. Then George handed me another package. TWO! I couldn't believe that Carolyn and George bought me <u>two</u> Christmas presents. I cried as I opened yet another beautiful dress. They all made me feel special. Though I missed Daddy, it was a good Christmas. Not because I got lots of presents, but because no one fought. Mama used to get drunk and complain about the presents Daddy bought her every year. For the first day in a long time, no one walked on eggshells. No one argued or hit another person.

After opening presents and visiting with relatives, Mama and I went to the bar to wish other friends, "Merry Christmas." Even that wasn't all that bad. Mama was lonely and I understood that she needed comforting from friends. Perhaps that was my Christmas present to her. For one day, I was compassionate about her needs and I loved her unconditionally. It was a good day.

57
Mama Remarried

Mama went away for the weekend and came home married to a man named Billy. He moved in with us right away. He drank even more than Mama did. It seemed that they were always either at the bar or getting drunk at home.

Mama wanted her step mother to meet Billy so we took a trip to Sanibel Island. On the way there, Billy wanted to stop at a liquor store to buy some booze. Mama and I waited out in the car as Billy went in. We waited and waited. We were in the car for a long time before Billy came back. Mama was mad that he took so long. She started yelling as Billy explained what delayed him. He opened up the grocery bag and inside was a small bottle of booze, a coke, and chips for me. Then he opened up his jacket and inside he had two more small bottles of booze. I couldn't believe it! He stole booze from the store. Mama was furious and immediately she told Billy what a bad example he was setting for me. I remembered once when George stole a stop watch from K-mart®, Mama made him take it right back in and return it. Why didn't she ask Billy to take the booze back in and return it?

Light Beyond the Darkness

58
There Was No Sign Of Life

After Billy and Mama were married, I spent much of my time with Tommie Lee. Mama and Billy not only drank a lot, but they fought a lot too. Butch was home from the Army but had moved out of the house. George moved away from home too. Tommie Lee's house was the only place for me to go. Though I was still tense about being around Uncle Bob, I figured out ways to avoid the situation. Besides, there were a lot of good things at Tommie Lee's and I could find ways for the good to out number the bad. I loved Aunt Marilyn and I loved being around her; that was one positive thing about Tommie Lee's. Another positive aspect of Tommie Lee's house was that every Sunday they went to the Baptist Church in Palmetto. I enjoyed that too.

One Sunday morning before church, I called Mama and Billy to find out what time they planned on picking me up, but no one answered the phone. Usually Uncle Bob took us out to brunch after church and since I couldn't get in touch with Mama, he and Aunt Marilyn decided to not to go for brunch. After returning to Aunt Marilyn's from church, George stopped by to pick up Eddie to go to the mall. Tommie Lee and I wanted to go to the mall so bad! At first, Aunt Marilyn said that Tommie Lee and I shouldn't go because she was afraid that my Mama would be mad at her if she drove all the way to Palmetto and I wasn't there. Then after a little thought she figured that Mama couldn't be too mad if I went with my brother George. I was hesitant to go too; because I scared of Mama also! I knew that Mama would kill me if she came all the way over to Aunt Marilyn's and I wasn't there. We tried to call Mama again and still there was no answer. Finally, we all agreed to be back at Aunt Marilyn's by 2:30 p.m.

At the mall, I continued to call Mama several times. There was no answer. Tommie Lee tried to get my mind off Mama by showing me all the neat places to shop. We tried on clothes, played video games at the arcade, and walked around with George and Eddie. I felt cool spending time with my older brother. Then Tommie Lee and I went one way and George and Eddie went another. We hung around the mall and before we knew it, it was 2:30 p.m. I began to worry because I had no idea where George and Eddie had wondered off too and I wanted to get back to Aunt Marilyn's. I called Aunt Marilyn's but the line was busy. Aunt Marilyn often took the phone off the hook because Uncle Bob worked evenings and had to sleep during the day. Tommie Lee tried to cheer me up and bought me an Orange Julius®. As we sat there drinking I kept my eyes opened for George. It wasn't long before I spotted him and ran after him.

"George, George, you have to take me back to Aunt Marilyn's! Mama is gonna pick me up and if I'm not there she's gonna kill me! Please, take me back!" George understood and we raced to his car. George drove back to Aunt Marilyn's as fast as he could. As we turned on to Snead Island an ambulance sped by us with its lights on, but no siren. I looked at Tommie Lee and said, "I bet whoever is in that ambulance is dead and that's why they don't have their siren on." I thought that was a weird thing to say but I didn't say a word because I was too worried that Mama would be mad.

We pulled into the driveway and Uncle Bob was walking out to his car to leave for work. I jumped out of the back seat and shouted, "Was Mama here yet?"
"Yes." Uncle Bob replied in a monotone voice.

"Where is she?" I asked in a panic.

"She left already. And well, she got in a car accident and, um, Billy's dead." Uncle Bob was very intelligent, but didn't have a way with talking to people.

"Are you kidding?" I asked.

Without looking at me, he replied, "No." As he spoke he got in his car and buckled his seat belt. "Where's Mama?" I cried.

George, Eddie and Tommie Lee were still in the car. They were waiting in the street for Uncle Bob to back out of the driveway. They didn't hear our conversation and had no idea what was going on. I stood in shock, still wondering if Uncle Bob was telling me the truth. Then he said out the car window, "She's in the hospital and they don't know if she's going to live."

I ran into the house and grabbed the yellow pages to call the two local hospitals. I called Manatee Memorial and asked if they had any record of Nancy Carolyn McCorkle being admitted. They couldn't find her. I hung up and Tommie Lee walked in. George and Eddie had left before they found out about the accident. Aunt Marilyn wasn't home so Tommie Lee and I were home alone. Waving my arms in the air, I ran down the road trying to flag them down. I wanted my brother. I wanted him to help me find Mama. He didn't see me and sped away. Instead of wasting any more time, I ran back inside to call the one other hospital and out about Mama.

As I called the emergency room at Blake Hospital, I tried to explain to Tommie Lee what Uncle Bob had told me. I explained to her that I couldn't tell if he was pulling my leg or telling me the truth. Wouldn't he have been a little more sympathetic if Mama was really in an accident? I was so confused but I had to find out for myself. Neither emergency rooms had a record of a Nancy Carolyn McCorkle. I had forgotten that Mama was just married and changed her last name. Her new last name was Barnett. Tommie Lee and I decided to walk the two miles to the canal where Butch and a guy named Lee lived on a house boat. No one was there. When we arrived back at Tommie Lee's house, exhausted and emotionally drained, I decided it was time to find my Daddy. Daddy didn't have a phone in his one-room efficiency, but I left a message at the motel. I called every bar in town and finally found him at Lopez Lounge, the bar across the street from his motel.

Early in the evening, around six o'clock, Daddy and his girlfriend came out to Aunt Marilyn's house. We sat around the dining room table as Daddy explained Mama's condition to me and what had happened in the accident. His girlfriend was very nice and cried more than I did as Daddy retold what happened.

Daddy said that Mama and Billy had been drinking and seemed to be arguing when they came to pick me up. When I wasn't at Aunt Marilyn's house, Mama got even more mad. In an angered state she recklessly drove to the end of Snead Island. It was a desolate place where only a few people went to fish and drink beer. Perhaps she was mad and wanted to go out there and wait until I returned from the mall. She probably didn't want to drive all the way back to Palma Sola. The curvy dirt road leading out to the end of the island was dangerous. When Mama got mad, she put the pedal to the metal. She was driving very fast and shortly after passing a truck, she lost control of her car. The witnesses in the truck said that her car flew off the road going about 60 miles per hour. After leaving the road, her little car hit the bottom of a tree then bounced about six feet into the air. The car flipped and landed upside down in a ditch filled with water. The men in the truck (who just happened to be paramedics) rushed over to the scene, and tried to fight the dust that remained stagnant in the air. Looking into the ditch they saw air bubbles coming from the driver's side of the car but they didn't see any sign of life coming from the passenger's side. They rescued Mama but couldn't get to Billy.

Mama had several broken bones, a concussion, and internal bleeding. She was in critical condition and the doctors weren't sure if she would live. There wasn't an autopsy performed on Billy. The paramedics thought his neck was broken. However, the paper said that Billy drowned. The paper also said that several beer cans were found floating in the ditch and inside the car. It was a miracle that I wasn't at Aunt Marilyn's when Mama and Billy came to pick me up, perhaps I, too, when have been involved in an accident. Or maybe there would've never been an accident if I had been at Aunt Marilyn's house.

Daddy and his girlfriend were very supportive and they even took me to the hospital to see Mama. When I arrived there, the nurses and doctors were busy working on her. I stood outside the closed curtain and listened to Mama scream in agony. She kept asking where Billy was. I felt pain inside, like I had never felt before for Mama. I wanted so much to comfort her yet, I turned and walked away. I just couldn't see her. I felt guilty. I felt that if I had just stayed at Aunt Marilyn's maybe Billy wouldn't have died. I didn't know if the pain I felt was because of Mama's agonizing cry of physical pain or if it was because Mama wanted to see Billy. Both hurt me and added to my guilt. I couldn't help but wonder if this was all my fault. There had been many times that I both had jokingly "wished" out loud for Billy to die. For some reason I resented him and his drinking. It wasn't a very funny joke now. I asked myself, over and over, if I really meant it when I said, 'I wish that Billy would die.'

In school, Mrs. Michealson, my substitute English teacher, brought in an article about Mama. As class was getting out, she called me over to her desk. She told me that she was very sorry about what happened. She wanted to let me know that she was praying for my mother's life. I had no reaction.

She asked, "Are you doing okay?"

I answered hesitantly, "Yea, I think so."

"Well, you just pray for your mom and she will be just fine." Mrs. Michealson assured me.

My shocking reply to her was, "I am praying... but not really for my mom to live, I'm praying that God will do what He thinks would be best."

Mrs. Michealson gave me an inquisitive look and I turned and left.

As Mama lay in that hospital, I just couldn't help but think that maybe, things would be better if Mama <u>didn't</u> live. I loved my Mama, but I couldn't forget all of the terrible things that happened in the past. I didn't want to pray that Mama would die, part of me didn't want her to die, so I prayed that God would do what He thought would be best.

Mama lived through the accident. She lost a lot of her eyesight, and part of her brain was damaged. There was talk that Mama was going to be charged with manslaughter for the death of Billy, because of the drinking and driving. However, Mama knew the police officer in charge of the investigation and no charges were ever brought forward.

59
Mama's Fourth Husband

Mama's first husband was Howard. Together they had Butch and George. Mama and Howard argued often and according to Mama, Howard couldn't keep a job. Mama left him while the boys were still young. They had some really rough times. Butch and George remember living out of an old car and having barely anything to eat. They said that my life was easy compared to theirs. Mama met Lorenzo Ray McCorkle at a bar. She got pregnant but didn't want to get married. Lorenzo threatened to commit suicide if she didn't marry him and that's when it became Mama, Daddy, Butch, George, and <u>me.</u>

Mama married for the fourth time. This time the man's name was Frank Anderson. He worked on a fishing boat. He had been in Vietnam. He usually wore black leather, smoked marijuana and drove a motorcycle, but for the most part he was okay because he left me alone.

Our house sold and we moved into a duplex in Oneco, Florida. We had to leave Baby with our neighbor when we moved because our new place didn't allow dogs. The only pet we kept was my loyal cat and companion, Tomcat.

Shortly after our move to Oneco, I met a lot of boys in our neighborhood. All of them were older than me and they were into marijuana and drugs. Mama and Frank smoked "pot" every day so when my new friends said they liked to smoke pot, I didn't think anything of it. I admitted to them that I had smoked in the past; however, it wasn't something I did every day.

213

We had great adventures during the summer I lived in Oneco. The television was broke and so I spent most of my time out on my ten-speed exploring. Sometimes, I would gather up the guys, David, Lloyd, Stretch and others to play in the nearby woods. No one ever had any money, although I wondered where they found money to buy drugs. Even though the question came to mind, I decided not to ask. I decided I would rather not know. Without money, we found other things to do. Occasionally, the guys, would just want to sit around and smoke pot, but I could usually talk them into doing other things. We would go into the woods and play army or even go swimming. There was a deep man-made hole near our house filled with dirty brown water, and for a lack of anything else to do, we would swim in it.

"Stretch" became my new boyfriend. His real name was Charles. He was tall and thin and that's where he got his nickname. Stretch had long dark brown hair and was very quiet. He never seemed to fit in like all the other guys. I felt sorry for him and I think that's why I liked him so much. Stretch smoked pot and even though I didn't mind the other guys doing it, for some reason, I didn't want Stretch to do it. I asked him to stop smoking it more than once. He promised he would never smoke around me and that he wouldn't smoke it before seeing me and I promised him that I wouldn't smoke pot at all. I thought that was a good arrangement.

On night as I lay in bed sleeping there was a tap at my window. It was Stretch. I didn't have a screen on my window so we found it easy for him to sneak in and out. After that night Stretch climbed in my bedroom window a lot. As we lay there in bed together we would kiss and whisper about our dreams. Sometimes we talked about getting married and having children. Once Stretch told me that he felt really bad at home. He didn't think he could do anything to please his mom. His father was gone. He really felt like his mother hated him. I didn't believe him until she called me one day. She told me that she thought that I was too good for her son. She told me that he was on some drug called Angel Dust, but when I asked Stretch if it was true he said, "No." Stretch knew that I wouldn't see him any longer if he did any drugs harder than alcohol and pot. Those to me, back then, were acceptable but nothing more.

I rarely saw Mama and Frank. They never asked me what I did. They let me do as I pleased. They thought that I was doing just fine. I was always home before dark and usually went to bed early (so Stretch could sneak in). Unlike Mama and Daddy, Mama and Frank spent a lot of their time together.

Stretch and I lay next to each other on my bed night after night and whispered our deep secrets. Sometimes, Stretch would ask me about my sexual experience and I was reluctant to talk about it. I was scared that he wouldn't like me anymore or maybe worse that he would take advantage of me. I remembered my previous experiences and didn't want to go through any of it again. Months went by and Stretch and I grew closer and closer. Eventually, Stretch begged me to prove to him how much I loved him. I finally caved in and it was another agonizing experience for me. Afterwards, Stretch never wanted to let me out of his sight, and for some reason, I lost all interest in him. I started liking Lloyd, one of the other boys that I hung out with.

Mark, Frank's oldest son stopped by our house one night. He often would come over to get high with Frank and Mama. This time however, before coming in to the house to visit, he took Stretch, Lloyd and I up to the store and bought beer for us. One the way back from the store I looked for the note to give Lloyd. I wanted him to read it that night because I was going out of town the next day. However, I couldn't find it. It must have fallen out of my back pocket and into the seat of the car. I asked Mark to turn on the over head light, but he said it didn't work.

Stretch asked what the note was about and I said, "Nothing."

When we got back to the house my Daddy was there waiting for me. Daddy was being transferred to Indiana and I planned on going there with him for the summer. Since Daddy was in the house, I forgot to look for the note and instead, bolted out of the car and ran in to see Daddy. Lloyd, Mark and Stretch stayed outside to have a drink. Mark and Lloyd came in a little later but Stretch stayed outside. I asked Mark where Stretch was and he told me that Stretch found a note from me to Lloyd and was outside reading it. "Oh no!" I thought to myself. I jumped up out of my chair and ran outside. There stood Stretch in front of Mark's car with the headlights on trying to read my long love letter to Lloyd. I tried to grab it out of his hands but it didn't matter, he had already read most of it. Tears were streaming down his cheeks and I felt terrible. I had no words to justify my actions. I had no defense for the ruthless way I had hurt him. I tried to apologize, but he didn't want to hear it. He took off down the road. I returned in to the house and tried to act cool even though I felt very foolish.

Soon after I returned in, Daddy said it was time to go. As we were all getting ready to leave, we heard a loud crash outside. We figured there must have been a fender bender out on the highway that we lived next to. We finished our good-byes and walked outside. As soon as we were out the door we realized that Stretch had stolen Mark's car <u>and</u> in the process crashed into Daddy's car rear fender. Mark had given Stretch his keys so that he could turn on the head lights and read the note. Daddy and I left and went on our way to Indiana although I was worried about Stretch the entire trip. Once we arrived I called home to Mama and found out that Stretch had run Mark's car off a bridge but he was okay. His mom put him in a juvenile detention center. I never saw him again after that night.

60
Summer in Crown Point, Indiana

Daddy and I stopped in Tennessee on our way to Indiana. All the motels were full so we ate dinner at a bar/restaurant where they played blue-grass music and then we spent the night in the car. Daddy woke up early and started to drive to Indiana. I slept for in for a while.

I was glad when we finally arrived in Indiana. Daddy lived in an adult apartment complex. Mid Valley had set up the arrangements for him to have the apartment but when we arrived there was no furniture or television. Right away, we went out and bought the basic necessities; a couch for me to sleep on and a bed and dresser for Daddy. Daddy said the television would have to wait till next payday. He had a clock radio so I could listen to music and there was a pool at the apartment complex. Since there wasn't really anything else to do, I spent almost every day out by the pool while Daddy went to work. Eventually, I met some friends. Unfortunately, they weren't even close to my age; they were all much older.

The lifeguard, Teri, who worked at the pool, was around 20 years old. She was outgoing and friendly. She and I became acquaintances; talking while I sunned at the pool. One day a guy wanted to meet me. He asked Teri to introduce us. Teri didn't really know me either so she invited me to play water volleyball with her and all the other people her age at the pool. We played for some time until the guy, who was also around 20 years old, asked me how old I was. I knew they thought I was older, so I asked them, "How old do you think I am?" They all thought I was around 18 years old. They were amazed when I told them the truth. Even though the guy had no interest in me after that as a "girlfriend," I still remained great friends with him and Teri. Teri didn't care that I was so much younger and started inviting me to do a lot of things with her. She gave me beer and took me to parties. I was a child but acted more like an adult. I went to adult parties; I spoke like an adult and most people had no idea what my real age was.

Daddy became suspicious of my behavior and decided it was time I had supervision. He called an old girlfriend of his Bonnie, to come up and visit and watch out for me. In the meantime, I noticed Daddy was getting sick. He was coughing a lot and sometimes he spit up blood.

Daddy smoked a lot, and he coughed when he went to bed. One night, he looked pale and he started coughing uncontrollably when tiny drops of blood came spurting out of his mouth. Daddy passed out and I was scared. Hysterically, I ran over to the neighbors and they were able to wake Daddy up. He said that he was just coughing too hard and didn't get enough oxygen. They wanted to take him to the hospital but he wouldn't go.

The next day, Daddy went to work as usual. Since he went to work, I figured he must have felt better. I called him and asked if I could go shopping with Teri. He said it was okay. Teri really wanted me to go to a party with her in Gary, Indiana. But I knew Daddy would agree to that. Teri and I drove to the but it was dead. The only people at the party were Teri, myself and the girl who lived in the apartment. We drank a couple of bottles of wine and those two smoked pot. Teri was so wasted she couldn't even drive home. She wanted to stay in Gary and sleep until she felt like she could drive but it was late and I couldn't stay any longer. I knew that I was going to get killed and was getting nervous about facing Daddy. I finally told Teri that I'd drive us home. Tommie Lee and I had driven Uncle Bob's truck a lot on Snead Island. I knew the basics. Though I had never driven more than a couple miles, I would rather drive home than sit and let Daddy get even more mad at me for staying out so late. The trip home was over an hour and at first I was okay. But soon I realized that I was way out of my league. Not only had I drunk too much wine, but, I didn't even have a permit. It was even a challenge trying to keep Teri stayed awake on the way home so that she could direct me where to turn. But we finally arrived at the complex safe and sound.

When Teri and I walked into my apartment, we saw Bonnie (Daddy's girlfriend) sitting on the floor. She was crying. She had a drink in one hand and a cigarette in the other.

"Oh, thank goodness your home. I've been worried sick about you," Bonnie said.

I couldn't tell who had more to drink Bonnie, Teri or me. But I felt better knowing that we were all drunk.

I apologized and started to tell my story when Bonnie interrupted, "It doesn't matter, I'm just glad you're home safe. Your Daddy is in the hospital. He almost died tonight."

"WHAT?!" I asked, as guilt rushed through my bones. I felt like I immediately sobered up.

Apparently, Daddy had a blood clot in his lungs. He had to be rushed to the hospital and they went right into surgery. Bonnie was afraid that Daddy wouldn't make it. Teri, Bonnie and I sat on our living room floor and cried. Finally, I laid my head on Bonnie's lap and fell asleep.

Daddy recovered and came home after a few days in the hospital. Bonnie stayed about a week and took care of him. She suggested to Daddy that I ride back to Florida with her on the train. She felt that it just wasn't good for me to stay in Indiana any longer. She was probably right. I rode the train back to Florida with Bonnie. Mama met us at the train station.

61

Returning Home   August, 1978

It was early August when I returned to Oneco. I was excited to see the boys and get back into some good old fun. Stretch was sent away but more than anything I wanted to see Lloyd, so I biked over to his house. He was there with his family. They lived in a small duplex like ours.

Lloyd and I went into his room and shut the door. I was amazed that his mom would let him in the room with a girl. He said that his mom didn't care what he did. Not long after entering his room, I made another grave mistake in my life and upon leaving Lloyd's house he said that he would call me. He never did. I felt so lonely. Never had I felt so depressed. Did anyone love me? I gave up Stretch for Lloyd. Stretch risked his life for me. He really loved me and now he was gone. I felt like the stupidest person on earth. How could I continue to make the same mistakes over and over. It was the worst feeling in the world.

.

62

Moving Again   August, 1978

It was time to move again and this time I <u>wanted</u> to move. I wanted to start over and begin again. I felt like I had made so many mistakes. I knew that what I had done both in Indiana (drinking and partying) and in Oneco (promiscuity) were wrong, and yet, it was so hard for me not to do those things. I couldn't understand why I would do the things that I hated to do the most? Why?

Romans 7:15 (TLB)

*I don't understand myself at all, for I really
want to do what is right, but I can't. I
do what I don't want to do-what I hate.
I know perfectly well that what I am
doing is wrong, and my bad conscience
proves that I agree with these laws I am
breaking. But I can't help myself,
because I'm no longer doing it. It is sin
inside me that is stronger than I am
that makes me do these evil things.*

I knew God didn't approve of my actions especially the promiscuity, yet, it was just so hard for me to say "No." I wanted someone to love me. I wanted someone to show me that they really cared about me. Why did it seem that love and caring always turned into sex?

Light Beyond the Darkness

63
St. Petersburg, Florida

Mama and Frank rented a house in St. Petersburg. It was in a bad part of town and the house wasn't in tip-top condition, but I liked it anyway. It had character. Upon entering the house, it appeared to be a maze. Though the house wasn't the smallest house we had ever lived in, it consisted of many small rooms. We used the front porch as our living room. Off the porch was an L-shaped hallway that led to the tiniest kitchen I had ever seen. The only thing in the hallway was my 40 gallon tropical fish tank and stand that I had saved up to buy when we lived in Palma Sola. A small closed up room sat mysteriously off the kitchen. I was allowed in there once when we first moved in. The walls were pink and within them were beautiful turquoise and white ceramic tiles. The small room had many windows (some were broken) and the sun shone in and made the room warm. If not for the cobwebs and broken glass, it could have been very cozy. It was the only room in the house that allowed so much sun to come in. All the other rooms, including Mama and Frank's bedroom, my room and the back porch had small windows that allowed a breeze but nothing else.

I liked my room even though it was small. It was in the back of the house across from the bedroom. Frank let me have a phone and his portable television and that kept me occupied most of the time. When I wasn't talking long distance to my cousin on the phone or watching television, I was out riding on my yellow ten speed. I wanted to meet new people and make new friends.

64

The White Witch   September, 1978

I met the lady who lived next door. She lived all alone and something seemed interesting about her. She was nice and introduced herself to me. Mama and Frank were always preoccupied; either they were at work, out on a motorcycle ride, at a bar, or sat watching television. So, I spent many afternoons with this unusual lady. She intrigued me with talk of fortune telling and witchcraft. As time went by she eventually she referred to herself as a "white witch." I had never in my life heard anyone refer to themselves as a "witch." Until then, I didn't even believe in witches. I thought they were something out of fairy tales. She assured me that she was a good witch and wouldn't harm me.

I began to ask Mama questions about witchcraft, without telling her about the lady next door. Mama told me that witches didn't believe in God. She told me that all witchcraft was from the devil. Mama told me to stop talking about such nonsense and so I quit asking her about it. I decided to tell the lady next door about Mama's viewpoint on witchcraft. She was very understanding, and told me that Mama was kinda right. She explained to me that there were actually two different kinds of witches. White witches were good and had the power to help people. She said that black witches were bad, they followed Satan and used black magic. I asked many questions. When I asked her about believing in God, she assured me that she did believe in God.

> *Deuteronomy 18:10-12(NIV)*
> *Let no one be found among you who sacrifices his son or daughter in the fire, who practices divination or sorcery, interprets omens, engages in witchcraft, or casts spells or who is a medium or spiritist or who consults with the dead. Anyone who does these things is detestable to the Lord, and because of these detestable practices the Lord your God will drive out those nations before you.*

Since the lady next door knew so much about witches and said she believed in God, I decided to trust her and believe her. I didn't know that the Bible warned us about witches and that all practices of witchcraft were detestable before God Holy eyes.

The witch's stories of helping others, and of a warlock she knew (who wasn't so nice) were interesting to me. One day, she lit candles, pulled out a Bible and placed a glass of water next to a strange deck of cards on the dining room table. I felt as if I was living in a mystery. Then she told me it was time to learn my future. She was drawing me in closer and closer to her world of wonder and intrigue. I shuffled the deck and she read the cards to tell me what she could see. She seemed to know so much about me.

It wasn't long before I received a gift from the lady next door. I was told to keep it a secret; it was two books that explained in great detail how to become a witch. Every day the lady next door encouraged me to read the books and to do as they said. She wanted me to read them in a hurry and explained to me why. There were only a few opportunities to become a witch during the year and there was much to do before the opportunity passed us by.

At first, I thought it would be neat to have her powers. I daydreamed about how I could've used those powers to heal Daddy when he was hurt and how I could use them to help my family be "normal." I enjoyed having the lady next door read my cards and I began to buy books about the cards she used. As much as the powers of witchcraft and telling the future sounded appealing, there were things that I had questions about. Such as why did I have to have a secluded altar that no one else could go to? What was the meaning of the circle and the star? Why do you have to worship at the altar <u>naked</u> and what was the meaning behind the little tiny book I was suppose to make and wear around my neck?

Acts 13:10(NIV)
Paul speaking to a sorcerer.
"You are a child of the devil and an enemy
of everything that is right! You are
full of all kinds of deceit and trickery.
Will you never stop perverting the
right ways of the Lord?"

As much as I wanted to help my family be "normal," I knew that one of the ten commandments was-*Thou shalt not worship any other gods.* I had a bad feeling about going to an altar naked because I had always associated the word altar with my acceptance of the Lord Jesus Christ. I knew that I didn't want to worship any other God. I tried to explain to the next door lady that I felt uncomfortable with building an altar and going there naked. I asked her if there was something else I could do instead. I told her that every time I thought of an altar I thought of church. She tried hard to convince me that I wouldn't be disobeying the commandment if I built a simple altar in my back porch where no one ever went. She tried to persuade me in to building the altar and she said that I would understand after it was all done. I continued to hesitate and she

229

became a little frustrated. She tried so hard to convince me that I was doing the right thing that she scared me. Instead of continuing , I gave her books back and soon afterwards we had a disagreement in which we never spoke again.

Today, I believe with all my heart it was the Holy Spirit that gave me the discernment to stop the process of becoming a witch. When I accepted Christ, the preacher told me that Jesus would never leave my side and Jesus confirmed that when he told his apostles that he was sending a messenger to them. That messenger is the Holy Spirit, He is given as a gift to help us along our way when we are born- again and accept Jesus as our Savior. I believe it was the Holy Spirit who helped me not turned to witchcraft.

65
The Perfect Family

A new family moved in across the street. They had a girl the same age as myself. Her name was Dawn. Her tall, medium build frame and shoulder length dark drown hair pretty made her very pretty. And her New York accent was really cool. She moved in shortly after we did and we seemed to have a lot in common. We both lived with our real mothers and step-fathers; we both recently moved to St. Petersburg; We both liked the piano and we both had big gray cats. Her cat was named Tom and mine was Tomcat. As soon as we met, we became friends. We took walks together and played games together. I taught Dawn what ever I could on the piano. She could play music that she had heard but had never had a lesson. She couldn't even read music. So I began to teach her how to read notes and the different keys on the piano. At first it was fun to share my talents with a friend but soon I realized that she without ever having a lesson was a much better pianist than myself. I became jealous.

One day Dawn's stepbrother, Peter came to live with them. Peter had curly brown hair and a nice physical appearance. He was having problems living with his mom in Arizona and came to Florida to stay with his real dad. He was a couple years older than Dawn and me. He and I bonded together quickly. I felt sorry for him and we seemed to understand each other. We rode bikes together and talked a lot about our pasts. Dawn and I began to see less and less of one another as I became more interested in Peter. Perhaps I let the jealously of the piano interfere with our friendship or maybe I just preferred the male attention.

Long before I met Peter, I had made the decision not to tell anyone about my history with guys. The loneliness that enraged me after saying "yes" too many times was too much for me to handle again. I just couldn't forget the misery I went through after giving in to something that I knew was wrong. I felt dirty and guilty. I didn't like the fact that the boys had lied to me about loving me, but that wasn't all. I felt really bad about doing something that I felt God didn't intend for me to do. I believe that's why I felt so guilty, so ashamed and so unworthy. I had over heard many people talk about how now in the 70's that it was okay to do that kind of stuff if you were in love. I wondered if God thought it was okay? I tried to convince myself that as long as your in love than it's okay. But deep down I knew that the guys that I was with didn't loved me.

Peter and I hung out together quite a bit, and eventually I got up the nerve to ask him if we were "boyfriend and girlfriend," and he said sure. Up until then our relationship was great but once I titled us "boyfriend and girlfriend" our friendship began to change. We began to talk less and to touch and kiss more. The changes bothered me because I knew where it was leading. Peter tried touching me in personal areas and soon timidity set in and I became very quiet and frigid when we were alone. I began making up excuses why I couldn't go on a bike ride or on a walk. It wasn't long before Peter said that I was 'nice and everything, but I just wasn't his type of girl.' Little did he know. I acted sad but in my heart I felt relieved. Peter shared with me on the phone when he was breaking up that even his dad couldn't understand why we hadn't slept together. I was surprised by that statement and asked Peter for clarification. Peter retold his dad's words, 'I can't believe you haven't gotten that girl in bed yet. Why with all the time she spends alone in that house of hers.'

After Peter and I broke up, Dawn and I still didn't regain our friendship. Perhaps she had too much resentment towards me for just leaving her out when Peter was around. Guilt again was eating me up inside and so one afternoon when there was nothing else to do, I called her and asked her to go on a walk. We started opening up again and that's when she shared with me that she and Peter were sleeping together. Late at night she would sneak into the living room where he slept on the couch. It became a game to her. It made me angry that it was so easy for her. Why did I feel so ugly, dirty and guilty when I said 'yes' to a boy. I didn't want to hang around Dawn or her family anymore. I didn't feel comfortable around her dad and lost respect for what I thought was the "perfect family."

Needless to say, I wasn't too sad when Peter was suddenly forced to go back to Arizona. When I saw Dawn at school she told me that she and Peter were caught together by her stepfather and he made Peter leave immediately.

Light Beyond the Darkness

66

Feeling Empty   October, 1978

I was embarrassed of Mama and Frank. The Bible told me to honor my Father and Mother but surely He didn't mean that to me. How could I honor them when did so many bad things. When I had a friend over, Mama would ask, "Are they cool?" That meant, would it be okay for her and Frank to smoke a joint in front of them. Of course none of my friends would mind, they thought my parents were very cool.

Mama and Frank didn't seem to care what I did either. There were barely any rules and my few friends thought that I had the ideal life. I, on the other hand, thought it was terrible. Parents weren't supposed to smoke pot and therefore break the law. Parents were supposed to set a good example. Mama lived by the rule, "Do as I say, not as I do."

I wanted real parents. I wanted parents that would ask me how my day went, or look at my homework or just pay attention to me. Mama and Frank gave me the necessities and they even paid for my piano lessons but there was no affection, no loving moments together. Nothing. Sometimes, I wondered what was worse, being totally left out and feeling neglected like with Mama and Frank, or having a mixture of really good days (like fishing and church) and really horrible days filled with hatred and violence. That's how it was with Mama and Daddy. But I guess for Daddy's sake it was better that they got a divorce.

With Mama and Frank drugs were the center of their life. I'll never forget the day that Mama was getting

235

dressed for work in the bathroom and she asked me to go get her bra. They were in the top middle drawer of her dresser. For some reason, I opened the <u>bottom</u> middle drawer of her dresser and there I saw hypodermic needles. It scared me. I shut the drawer fast and acted as though I had seen nothing. Then I recalled seeing a similar needle back in Oneco when our toilet was backed up and the plumber pulled the same type of needle out of the pipes. Mama said that she thought it probably belonged to the neighbors (we lived in a duplex).

So many years have gone by since the days of feeling empty. God has now filled me with His grace and reassurance. God knew what He was doing when he gave the parents that He did. He had a perfect plan and years after the abuse ended, I came to realize what God meant when He said to Honor thy Father and Mother. I searched but no where in the Bible did God say Honor thy Father and Mother when they are good, when they obey my commandments. He didn't say to Honor them whey they honored Him. He said to Honor them always. My praise and glory go to God for giving me a merciful heart so that I could seek His forgiveness for not always honoring my parents. I praise him for giving me the parents that He choose for me. I think of God, who so mercifully allows us to call out to Him though we stray and how He tells us to be that very same example to all those we encounter. We need to love everyone as Jesus does.

67

Panic   November, 1978

Mama called to tell me that Frank would be home early from work. She didn't fully trust Frank around me. She was fearful that he would try something terrible on me if he were drunk or stoned. Mama told me to always be careful around him and to let her know if he ever did tried anything. She said she would kill him if he did, and I believed her.

Every day, I practiced the piano after school and the day that Frank was supposed to come home early was no exception. As I practiced, I kept a close eye out for Frank. My plan was that when I heard his motorcycle, I would go into my room and shut the door or go out for a bike ride. After an hour passed I became confused; Frank was supposed to be home early and now he was late. Frank must have stopped at a bar on the way home. One hour passed...two hours...three hours. Finally, I started to worry. I wasn't worried about Frank's safety; I was worried about Mama. Now Mama was late coming home too. I went into the kitchen to make my own dinner. There wasn't much to eat. I fixed myself a sandwich and a bowl of leftovers for dinner. I sat down and turned on the television wondering if I should call the police. What would I say, my parents are missing? Mama probably stopped at the store to pick up something to eat or at the bar to pick up some beer.

The phone rang. It was Mama. By the tone of her voice and the loud background noise, I knew she was at a bar.

She yelled into the phone, "Cheri, Are you okay? Is Frank there?"

I <u>felt</u> like yelling at her, but I knew better than that. Here I was worried about her safety and all along she was at the bar.

"No." I said, "Where are you?"

She didn't answer my question but instead began to speak louder into the phone. I heard panic in her voice, "Get out of the house. Frank's gone crazy!"

I was bewildered, "What do you mean, 'Frank's gone crazy?'" I could tell she had been drinking and immediately I began to doubt her words.

Mama was growing impatient and almost hysterical, "Frank called me from the bar. When I got off work, I met him here. Cheri, he was acting crazy and when I asked him if he was on drugs, he went hysterical and tried to kill me right here in the bar! Cheri, you have to listen to me. Frank is on his way home and you have to get out of there now!" For some reason, I knew that Mama was serious. Her concern was not for herself, it was strictly for me. She wasn't trying to get sympathy but instead she sounded as though she was trying to protect me.

I hung up the phone, grabbed Tomcat and ran across the street to Dawn's house. I didn't know where else to go. Crying, I told Dawn's mom what had happened and she was very understanding and compassionate.

Moments later, I heard Frank's motorcycle. As I looked across the street, I saw him drive into our yard. He jumped off his bike and ran up to the door. When it wouldn't open he started banging on it. I had locked the door when I left and Frank didn't have a key. He screamed, Open the f---- door! We could hear him from across the street as he continued to yell. Frank started walking around the house. I suppose he was checking the back door to see if it was open. I knew it wasn't. I always kept the house locked up because I was afraid to be alone. Frank finally gave up and came back around to the front door. The next time I looked out to see him, he was rocking back and forth on the front step. Then he laid down and curled up into a ball on his side. I knew he was on drugs and calling the police or an ambulance never even occurred to me. Instead I backed away from the window, I didn't know what to do. I started to cry and Dawn's mom closed the curtains and tried to comfort me. She suggested that Dawn and I play a game in her room. As we did I began to forget all about Frank.

Eventually Mama called Dawn's house and I told her that I was okay but that Frank didn't look so good. She told me that she didn't feel safe going home yet, so she was going to stay at the bar for a while. She told me to ask Dawn's mom if I could spend the night. Mama said that she would call me in the morning when it was safe for me to go home.

I didn't want to ask Dawn's mom if I could stay over. I didn't know anyone else whose parents lived this way. Why me? I wasn't sure if I trusted Dawn's dad, and I wasn't even that good of friends with Dawn anymore. I didn't have anything of my own to even sleep in and yet, I was too afraid to go home. What was I supposed to do? With my head lowered to the ground I walked up to Dawn's mom telling her that my mom didn't feel safe and asked if I could stay with them over night. She graciously agreed and continued to be loving and supportive. All night, Dawn and I sat up talking and when I finally went to bed, Mama still wasn't home. That night when I said my prayers I didn't pray for the safety of Frank or Mama. I selfishly prayed for me. I prayed that Dawn wouldn't tell anyone at school about what happened. That was my main concern...me.

The next morning when I awoke Frank's motorcycle was gone and Mama's car was parked in the yard. Mama had not called to say it was safe to come home but I needed to get ready for school. I called home...no answer. I waited and tried again... no answer. I hung up and called again, now worried about why Mama wasn't answering the phone. Tears filled my eyes as I dialed the number again. Mama still didn't answer the phone. Immediately, I knew, "There's something wrong." Every bad thing possible went racing through my mind as I gathered up Tomcat and ran across the street. What would I find at our house? Would Mama even be alive or would I find Mama murdered by her deranged husband? Perhaps Mama was just too hung over to answer the phone? I had no idea, but I had to find out.

The door was unlocked and when I threw it open, I found our house in a uproar. There was obviously a fight. Furniture was thrown across the room. Glass covered the floor. The television was even turned over on its side. As I entered into our long hallway I saw my fish tank. Glass and water were all over the floor. I shouted, "My fish!" Most of my fish lay motionless on the floor. I still didn't know if Mama was dead or alive, yet, for some reason, all I could think of was myself. The thought of her being murdered or laying dead on her bedroom floor, didn't even enter my mind. All I wanted to do was blame Mama for my dead fish, even if she didn't do it, I knew she was to blame. Mama always told people it was Daddy's fault when they got in a fight. Mama never took the blame. I knew otherwise and I wasn't about to believe anything she said, if she was alive.

I ran into Mama's room screaming with anger and pain, "How could you...?" I stopped dead in my tracks when I saw her. Her face was swollen and blue; her naked body was covered in black and blue marks and it looked as though this was one fight she didn't win. A dark line around Mama's neck indicated that Frank had tried to strangle her.

"Mama?" I whispered, wondering if she would even answer or if she were really dead. "Mama?" I whispered again, now with a little more fear in my voiced.

She moaned. I walked closer and bent down next to her bed. "Oh Cheri, he tried to kill me." she whispered so low that I could hardly hear her. For an instant I felt sorry for her, I could tell it hurt her to speak. Then I remembered all the incidences with Daddy. How many times had she tried to kill Daddy? I thought to myself, "She deserved this." I stood up and backed away from her bed. I was angry. The only things I could think of were the horrible injustices that she had put me through. She lay there on the bed. She could barely talk, and I had no sympathy for her whatsoever.

She needed comfort, perhaps even medical help. But all I could think was that she wanted me to feel sorry for her. She said, "Oh Cheri, he went crazy. Oh, Cheri, it was terrible." I just sat there and thought to myself, "You think everyone is terrible but you. It's about time someone beat you at your own game."

Instead of telling Mama what was going through my mind, I asked, "How did my fish tank get broken?"

She rubbed her neck, "Oh Cheri, look at my neck, he tried to strangle me."

"Oh, I see that. What happened to my fish tank?" was all I could say.

She opened her eyes just slightly, looking at me in surprise, "Frank did it. He threw the phone at me and it went through your fish tank. Oh Cheri, it was so horrible."

"Mama, I'm gonna go try and save the fish that aren't dead yet. Do you need anything?" I inquired with no sympathy for her physical state. I could tell that my tone of voice and lack of compassion irritated her. She told me to get her asked me to get her aspirin and water and added a sarcastic remark about 'your precious fish.'

241

When I finally got to my fish, I realized that few had survived. Most of the fish were flushed out of the tank through the large hole that the phone apparently had made. However, not all the water had drained out and a few of the smaller fish were swimming around the telephone that lay at the bottom of the tank. After cleaning up the glass and dead fish from the floor, I checked in on Mama. She was sound asleep. I looked at Mama and decided that I just couldn't deal with this all by myself. Quietly, I slipped out of the house and ran over to Dawn's to use the phone.

Butch was out of the Army. He lived in Bradenton and even though it was long distance, without any hesitation I asked Dawn's mom if I could call him. Normally I would have been to shy to ask anything, but I just felt as the end of my rope. Dawn's mom agreed that I should call my brother. I told Butch that Frank and Mama were in a fight. The house was destroyed and Mama was really hurt. Butch was immediately worried about Mama and me. He assured me that everything was going to be okay and that he would drive up as soon as he could get some help. At first, I didn't want Butch to come up to St. Petersburg. Mama would probably get mad at me if she found out that I told Butch about the fight. Yet, I didn't want to be alone with her all day either. I told Butch he didn't have to come but he insisted. What I didn't realize was that he thought Mama and Frank were still in the middle of a fight and that's why he insisted. He thought that he was driving up to save our lives, (a little misunderstanding on both our parts) so he wanted to get George and Eddie to help him break it up. I didn't think to tell him that the fight was last night and that Frank had already left.

By the time Butch, George and Eddie got to St. Petersburg (over an hour later), Mama was out of bed and in the bathroom, she was very sick (I'm not sure if it was from the fight or the booze). I had stayed outside as much as possible because Mama was already mad at me but she was also in a bad mood from last night. When Butch pulled in the yard and found out that Frank wasn't even there, he got a little mad at me. He told me that Mama was really going to kill me when she found out that I blabbered everything over the neighbor's phone to him. The boys sat in the car wondering if they should leave before Mama even noticed that they were there. I didn't tell them that Mama was irritated at me for not being more compassionate, I knew they would say that I deserved it. Instead, I just begged them to stay and didn't offer any reason why. I clutched Butch's car window in fear that they would drive off and leave me. I hung onto the car and refused to let them go. Reluctantly, Butch got out of the car and went in the house. When he saw all the damage caused to the house, he didn't seem as mad at me anymore. He called George and Eddie inside. He knew that there was a <u>serious</u> fight and I think he understood my fear. By the time Butch came in, Mama was back in bed and when Butch entered Mama's room, he couldn't believe his eyes. He had never seen Mama as beaten up and battered as she was that day.

As Mama cried and told Butch what had happened during the fight, Butch showed great sympathy and compassion. He was exactly what Mama needed and she was glad that he had come. At first she didn't even ask why he was there, she was just thankful that he was. Mama told Butch that Frank stopped beating her because the police came up. He took off on his motorcycle.

When Mama finally asked why Butch had come to the house, he told her that I had called him because I was afraid that Frank would come back. He didn't tell her that I called from the neighbor's house. Mama understood my fear and suggested that I go back to Bradenton with Butch and stay there until things settled down. Mama told me to pack up several clothes because she didn't know how long it would be. She said that if she ever saw Frank again she would kill him and that she wanted me to go somewhere safe.

68
Living with Butch   November, 1978

Living with Butch and his girlfriend Kay was a good experience. Butch and Kay lived in the upstairs of a duplex. The place had two bedrooms and was very cute. Butch and Kay had very little money and soon after I moved in the telephone was turned off. That was a big inconvenience for me but I never complained to my brother. He was doing all he could for me and I really liked living there. Every night when Kay came home she and I would make dinner. Butch and I usually had Hamburger Helper and Kay would eat a salad or a grapefruit. (Even though she was very thin, she was always on a diet.) Occasionally, Butch would buy steaks and then Kay would eat with us too. When I left St. Petersburg, the only things I had brought with me were Tomcat and some clothes. I didn't have any games or toys, but I had fun with an old bike that Butch fixed up for me and listening to their record player. I would listen to the album Jesus Christ Superstar or Bob Seeger's Nightmoves® over and over. I pretended to be a singer and memorized every word of my favorite songs. I rarely spoke to Mama after that day I left St. Petersburg. Without a phone it was difficult for her to contact us and vice versa.

Butch enrolled me in school at Hardee Middle School. It was architected just like my old school Sugg. Both schools were built in the same format and it made getting around pretty easy. However, though I knew the school format, I felt like an outsider. The kids wanted to know why I moved and why I lived with my brother. I had a hard time adjusting in school and didn't catch on too well.

Butch was much more strict than Mama. He had lots of rules. I couldn't go out and do something both Friday and Saturday night. Each weekend I had to choose which night I wanted to go out.

Tommie Lee and I started doing a lot together on that one night during the weekend. Butch would drop us off at the local teenage disco, called "The Classroom." There we would dance and flirt with boys. It was fun. It had the atmosphere of a bar but they didn't serve alcohol. Looking back, I know that The Classroom wasn't a healthy place for me to hang out. It was an atmosphere that encouraged promiscuity. Eventually, I met a young man with a Spanish accent, named Gilbert. He was a little older than me and a very good dancer. His parents worked in a local Grove picking oranges. Butch thought that since Gilbert could drive he was too old for me. One Friday night, instead of going to the Classroom with Tommie Lee, I asked Butch if I could spend the night with a friend I met at the disco whose name was Maria. Butch agreed. What I didn't tell Butch was that Maria was Gilbert's younger sister, so I was really going to spend the night at Gilbert's house.

I arranged for Maria and Gilbert's mom to pick me up when I knew that Butch wasn't going to be home. They lived out past Palmetto and as we drove the twenty minutes to get to their home, I began to feel guilty for lying to Butch. He had done so much for me. He was the only "parent figure" that ever cared about my school work and who ever showed me real love and attention. As we pulled into the yard, I saw the small wooden broken-down house and I really wondered if I had made the right decision by coming there. The paint was faded and peeling. The porch didn't look safe to stand on and some of the windows were broken out. For a split second, I wanted to call Butch and ask him to come pick me up, but I knew he would be furious when he found out I had lied. What if he made me move back to St. Petersburg to live with Mama? As my Daddy used to say, "I had made my own bed, now I had to lie in it."

Next to the house sat a trailer that seemed to be in better condition than the house. That was where Gilbert's aunt and her children lived. Gilbert's mother, a young short Spanish accented and heavier woman was very sweet. She took me in as if I were one of her own children. The adults were going out that night, so she instructed Maria and me to make dinner for the rest of the kids. We fried chicken and made fried tortillas. I felt like I was married and had a family. The fun lasted until that night when Maria and I lay in bed talking. She told me that Gilbert wanted me to go into his room to say goodnight.

I went into his room happy and innocent. I left feeling guilty. I felt so guilty and so ashamed that the next day, I went home first thing in the morning and I told Gilbert that I never wanted to see him again. If only I hadn't lied... none of this would have ever happened.

In the next few weeks, my mind wondered with worries of being pregnant. I prayed that I would die so that I wouldn't have to disappoint Butch. I couldn't bear to tell him that I may be pregnant. He had a bad temper and though I never feared him hitting me, I didn't want to upset him. I prayed that I wouldn't be pregnant. Eventually, the time came when I found out that I wasn't pregnant. I made a promise to myself that I would never have sex again until I got married. There was too much pain involved. Too much worry.

Light Beyond the Darkness

69
Torn Between The Joy of Christmas and The Feeling of Being Abandoned
December, 1978

Christmas at Butch's was very special to me. Kay decorated the Christmas tree and even though there was very little money to buy presents, it was a very warm and loving Christmas. Butch and Kay did everything they could to make my holiday memorable.

Daddy came to Butch's to visit me on Christmas. He bought me a beautiful pair of boots. He didn't give expensive presents very often so that too was very special. Then Daddy told me that soon he would be moving to Texas. He asked if I wanted to go with him. My only response was, "I don't know." But what I meant was "No." I just didn't want to hurt Daddy's feelings.

Shortly after Daddy left, Mama came over to visit. She asked me to go outside on a walk with her. We had a nice walk together until she told me that it was time for me to move out of Butch and Kay's. She told me that Butch and Kay needed time alone. They were thinking of getting married and that it just wasn't working out for me to live with them. I felt very confused. I thought it was working out fine. Was I causing problems for Butch and Kay? Suddenly I felt so out of place everywhere I went.

Mama told me that she and Frank had gotten back together and that I could go back and live with them, but things weren't going well between them. She wanted to leave him but didn't know where she was gonna go. Mama suggested that I move out to Texas and live with Daddy.

Though I loved Daddy, I didn't want to go live with him. I didn't want to move out of the state of Florida. Another reason I didn't want to live with Daddy was because except for our trip to Indiana, I had hardly seen him after the divorce. Even before the divorce I rarely saw him because he worked so much. Though I loved him very much, he was more like an unseen hero than a father to me. Mama always accused me of putting him on a pedestal. And I did put Daddy on a pedestal. Since I rarely saw Daddy, I never saw the things that she accused him of doing. I only saw what she did wrong. I loved him but I didn't want to go. The day started out with so much joy and when it ended I felt so abandoned.

70
Moved to Texas

Texas. I thought that kids in Texas would be riding horses to school and tying them up at the corral. Much to my surprise, Texas wasn't like that at all. Instead it was similar to Florida. The weather was especially similar. The people, however, seemed much different. Each time I had moved in Florida, I felt like I didn't fit in. It seemed as though I had to prove myself in order to be somebody's friend. In Texas, strangers would say, "Hi" as you passed them on the street. At school, the kids would come up to me and ask, "Hey, you must be new? Where're ya'll from?" It was a very easy place to meet new friends.

However, one similarity to Florida was that in Texas alcohol and sex were popular amongst the kids my age. In my eighth grade class, many girls would brag about how many times they had "done it" with their boyfriends. It was common talk. No one was ashamed or felt guilty.

Although I knew I shouldn't lie, I told everyone that I was a virgin. Though virgins were known as nerds, I decided I would rather be a nerd than to feel trapped into having sex. Despite how glamorous they all made it sound, I knew in my heart that it wasn't. I didn't want to feel the guilt and shame that always came to me after giving in to a boy.

Daddy and I lived in a two-bedroom trailer. I liked it and thought it was nicer than some of the houses I had lived in; so I wrote home to my family in Florida and told them of our luxurious living accommodations. Later,

Daddy bought a small three-bedroom home in Cove, Texas. Which was in the same school district as our trailer in Boumont. The little house was old and didn't compare to our new house in Palma Sola but it had character and I liked it too.

Living with Daddy was much different than I expected. In Florida, I never <u>really</u> knew Daddy because he and I never really talked. Whenever we were together as a family, Daddy was usually quiet. The only times I remember him talking were at the dinner table when he would tell us stories about work. Daddy never talked much about his childhood or about his dreams or hobbies. He kept to himself and even though we lived in the same house, I grew up admiring him from a distance.

Moving to Texas gave Daddy and me that time to bond together as a family. He was sweet and very caring. I found out that Daddy had a very difficult childhood. He taught me a lot as we learned to live with one another. He taught me about forgiveness. Daddy had a rough childhood. His parents died when he was young and his younger sister and brother often teased him. He loved them anyway and never spoke an ill word of them. Rarely would Daddy even speak a negative word about Mama. Even though she had hurt him physically and emotionally, he loved her long after they were divorced. Moving to Texas gave me an opportunity to grow close to a parent I hardly knew. Never once when I lived with Daddy in Texas did he spank me or hit me. When I was caught doing something wrong, Daddy would sit me down, give me a good talking to and usually take away the privilege that I wanted the most. His disappointment in me seemed like the worst punishment of all. Daddy believed that I could do well in school. Because of his encouragement, I tried harder and made good grades. Daddy believed in hard work and he lived by that rule. He put his all into everything he started. He believed that I could be a doctor and he encouraged me often.

Even though living with Daddy gave me an opportunity to know him better, things weren't always great. Daddy worked a lot and still frequented the local bars. I began to recognize that Daddy drank as much as Mama did, if not more! Yet it didn't bother me that he drank because Daddy never got angry or mean after drinking. Looking back, I now believe he used work and alcohol to subdue the pain he faced early in life when his parents died and his brother and sister teased him, and also because of his failed marriage to Mama.

Coming home from school each day, I found that I had a lot of time alone and soon began to hang out with the local guys in my neighborhood. The guys were nice but they liked to drink a lot. It seemed as though every where I went alcohol followed. Back then, I didn't mind it so bad, and to be accepted by the guys; I drank right along with them.

71
Black Magic February, 1979

I met a new friend at school. Her name was Sherry. She was in one of my classes and seemed like a nice girl. One day she invited me to spend the night at her house. I was reluctant at first. I had never met her parents and was pretty shy, even a little scared. Through my experiences, I had learned not to trust adults. However, I didn't want Sherry to make fun of me for being scared. So I told her that my Daddy was pretty strict and that he probably wouldn't let me. Sherry pleaded with me to ask Daddy and so I asked. That was my downfall: peer pressure. Daddy asked several questions about who would be home, then he agreed to let me spend the night.

Sherry lived on an isolated dirt road where there was only one other house. As Daddy drove us to her home, Sherry nudged me and made a scary face as we drove past her neighbor's house. "What?" I asked, wondering what she was trying to tell me. She shook her head no, and whispered, "I'll tell ya later."

Upon arrival, Daddy got out of the car and met Sherry's mom. She seemed nice and said that I would be in good hands. She made us hamburgers for dinner and then said we could play inside or outside.

We decided to play in the yard with Sherry's new puppy and then we watched television. After her parents went to bed, Sherry and I went into her room. Sherry slowly shut the door, and motioned for me to be quiet. She pulled out a small box and inside was a hypodermic needle and a bottle of liquid. Sherry looked at me, raised her eyebrows and asked if I wanted some. She surprised me by asking; I looked at her and faked a laugh. I had no idea what she was doing. I had a great uncle that was diabetic, and I thought Sherry might be also. But instead of asking, I assumed she was teasing and said, "No." She pleaded with me. This time I was definitely scared and didn't know if she was serious or teasing. One thing I knew for sure was that no peer pressure was going to get to me to put a needle in my arm. I refused. I quietly opened the bedroom door and walked out. I was very frightened. I thought to myself, "What did I get myself into this time?"

When Sherry came out of the room she said she had a great idea. I was skeptical of any "great idea" she might have had, but I wanted to get off the subject of what happened in the bedroom and agreed to listen. Sherry said that her neighbor who lived up the street was very interesting. She thought that I may want to meet her. I asked if her parents minded if we went up the road to the house after dark. Sherry assured me that they didn't mind and that her parents let her do almost anything that she wanted.

We went up the block. I was scared of the dark, so Sherry held my hand. She made a few cracks about me being so timid. At first, I was defensive but Sherry soon had me laughing with her. She had a way of making people laugh.

We arrived at the house and rang the doorbell. A woman about 21 years old answered the door.

"Hey Sherry! Come on in? Who's your friend?" said the woman.

I looked at her. My mind was racing with negative impressions as I glanced at her jet black hair and eyebrows. They were obviously dyed darker than her natural color. Her look was intriguing, yet, as I glanced at her to tell her my name, I noticed a strange look in her eyes. It was as though she had great interest in me. An interest that made me feel uncomfortable.

"Hi...I'm Cheri."

"Cheri, that's a pretty name, I'm Susan."

"It's nice to meet you." Mama and Daddy had drilled this statement into me so many times, I said it without even thinking.

Susan invited us into her small kitchen where she had just made fresh chocolate chip cookies. Sherry and I sat at the bar with a glass of cold milk and warm cookies. I enjoyed the hospitality and felt guilty for the thoughts of judgment that had previously run through my mind. I had judged Susan as someone evil by the way she dressed and looked. Now I sat in her kitchen enjoying cookies and milk. I was dead wrong, or at least that's what I thought.

Susan asked many questions about me. She said that I didn't sound like a typical Texan. I told her how I had just moved to Texas from Florida. Susan asked me lots of questions and we talked for a while. The entire time, Sherry was quiet. She just sat there staring, doing and saying nothing at all. She seemed to be off in another world until suddenly she piped in and said out of nowhere, "Susan, Cheri used to know a witch in Florida."

I had told Sherry about the experience in St. Petersburg with my next door neighbor, but suddenly felt very uncomfortable with Sherry blurting it to someone I hardly knew. Most adults didn't believe in witches and would probably accuse me of lying. I didn't feel like defending my past experiences with a perfect stranger. Susan, however, just raised her eyebrows, looked at me and said, "How interesting." She didn't ask any questions at all. Instead, she changed the subject and later asked if we would like to play a game. I said, "Sure."

Susan left the room and came back with a game I had never heard of before. It was called, "Ouija." I asked, "What is this?" as Susan began to take it out of the box. Sherry spoke up again. "It's a Ouija board. You use it to speak to the dead. They can tell you things about the past, present, and future." Sherry then proceeded to explain how the spirits would guide our fingers across the board. I laughed and told them that I didn't believe in ghosts and that I thought it was more likely our own hands that would be guiding our fingers. Susan looked up at me. She stared directly into my eyes for what seemed like eternity. "You have so much potential. You could have much power, Cheri. I will make the spirits come and then perhaps you will believe." Susan said very confidently. I sat there not knowing what to say. My heart began to pound and for a split second, I felt like I was in great danger.

Susan interrupted the silence, "Cheri, you knew a witch once. Was she a black witch or a white witch?" I was amazed that this adult knew about witches. I spoke up, but my voice seemed to quiver, "A white witch."
"Well, perhaps that is why you are so full of disbelief; white witches contain very little power compared to black witches." Sherry interrupted, "Susan is a black witch."
"Oh," was all I could say. I didn't know what to do. I knew from my previous experience that black witches performed black magic. They were supposedly the bad witches and white witches were supposed to be good witches. I didn't want to ask Susan if she was a bad witch or a good witch. I decided to go along with the game and I said a little prayer to myself, "God, help me out of this one."

We played with the Ouija board and Susan asked it a lot of questions about me. Most of the questions were pertaining to whether I had been reincarnated. I didn't even believe in reincarnation but, according to the board, I had been. The board came up with the name Rebecca, and that was supposed to have been my previous name. Then Susan asked a peculiar question. She asked if there were any spirits with us. Our hands moved to the word,

YES. I felt extremely tense when Susan asked the names of the spirits that surrounded us. Our fingers began circling the board and I wondered to myself if it was Sherry or Susan pushing the pointing device because I was barely touching it. It began to move faster and faster and suddenly flew off the board. At the same time every light in the house went out.

It was just like being in a bad storm when the electricity goes out, but this was even worse. For less than a minute we all sat there. Then Sherry got up and said she would go check the fuse box to see if a fuse had blown. The fuse box was outside under the carport. Susan walked out the front door as my heart pounded with fear. I thought that a burglar was going to step in any minute. I didn't want to move because I was afraid someone would grab me, yet I didn't want to sit there and wait to be grabbed.

> *Leviticus 19:31 (NIV)*
> *"'Do not turn to mediums or seek out spiritists, for you will be defiled by them. I am the Lord your God.'"*

"Sherry, are you scared?" I whispered. Sherry answered, "Yea, kinda." "Sherry, has this ever happened before?" I whispered again, hoping that this was a joke and not really happening. As she started to answer, we both stopped and listened. At first, I thought I was imagining it. No, it was definitely real. It sounded like a pack of dogs, or wolves howling somewhere outside. Sherry had a puppy, but this definitely wasn't him. That's when I thought to myself, "Enough is enough." Not even thinking, I jumped up and headed for the door. Hoping that Susan wasn't standing right outside, ready to grab me, I busted out the door and ran down the road as fast as I could. I didn't look back but heard someone running after me. I reached Sherry's door, ran in and grabbed the phone to call Daddy. Seconds later, Sherry ran in the door. She had followed me down the road and even though she was as fearful as I was, she begged me not to call my dad. I was just too scared and called him anyway.

Thank the Lord, Daddy was at home. Crying, I asked him to please come pick me up. At first, he was angry and refused to come. But I pleaded and begged and finally he said that he would. It took Daddy over an hour to arrive at Sherry's. It seemed like forever.

I never told him about the witch. I knew I would get in trouble for sneaking out of Sherry's house. I told him about Sherry's drugs and how that scared me and he was actually grateful that I had called him. Sherry and I rarely talked at school after that. We never spoke of that evening again.

72
The Truth

Daddy bought a garage just a couple of blocks from our house and turned it into a bar. He made it really nice and put pool tables in and everything. When he wasn't at his job, he was at the bar. On my 14th birthday, he took my boyfriend, Wayne, and me to the movie and dropped us off. Wayne was one of the guys that hung out around my neighborhood. He was into drinking, baseball, adult magazines and body building. We had been dating for a while. Daddy went back to the bar after dropping us off.

Wayne had brought a small bottle of Wild Turkey whiskey into the movie theater and we drank most of the bottle. When the movie was over, Daddy was supposed to pick us up. After the movie I became frightened because I had drank so much of the Wild Turkey that I was actually drunk and I knew Daddy would kill me if he found out. One of Daddy's favorite sayings was "Do as I say, not as I do."

I wondered to myself, why did I drink when I knew that Daddy was coming to pick me up? I was trying to be "cool", but it was actually a very dumb thing to do. Scared to death of what Daddy would do when he found me intoxicated, I waited for him to pick us up. We waited and waited and finally, I called home. No one was home. I called the bar and Daddy was there. He had forgotten all about us, and from the sound of his voice on the phone, he had had a few too many to drink as well. He finally arrived at the theater and told us that he would take us back to the bar to have a pizza. He never noticed that I was drunk or that I had even been drinking.

At the bar I developed quite a headache and all I really wanted to do was go home to bed. After pizza, I told Daddy I was tired and wanted to go home. He drove Wayne home and then dropped me off at our house. Daddy went back to the bar. I went right to bed feeling a little sick to my stomach. Some time after I fell asleep, I awoke to someone tapping on my window. It was Wayne. He had snuck out of his house, rode his bike over to mine and now wanted to sneak in my window. I let him in and we laid in my bed together. I was so tired all I wanted to do was lay there and fall asleep but I was too scared that Daddy would come home and find Wayne and me laying in bed together. So, Wayne and I laid there talking for a while, then we began to kiss.

Once again, I made a terrible mistake. I cried all night after Wayne left. Though we dated and continued to do what I felt was wrong, I thought that I loved him and that he loved me. I wondered over and over in my mind: if two people loved each other, was it okay for them to have a physical relationship? I tried to justify my actions. I thought that maybe God would catch up to the times and let people that were in love do those things. Many years later, and many mistakes later, I found out the truth:

> *I Corinthians 7:2 (KJV)*
> *To avoid fornication, let every man have his own wife, and let every woman have her own husband.*

> *I Corinthians 6:18 (KJV)*
> *He that committeth fornication sinneth against his own body.*

Romans 8:8 (KJV)
They that are in the flesh cannot please
God.

Looking back, I know that fornication was a sin that kept me in bondage for many years. Even though I had asked Jesus into my heart, I still made drastic mistakes. I wasn't prepared to fight against the evil in the world, and therefore, I fell in defeat. As I grew older, I continued to make the same mistake. The guilt and shame grew stronger and so did my bondage to sin.

Daddy never caught Wayne and I together, but he must have suspected something, because he decided that I was spending too much time alone at home and that I needed some type of supervision. He called Bonnie and asked her to come stay with us. He also offered her a job as bartender. She agreed and moved out to Texas with her three boys. Bonnie was a sweet southern woman. But she was also quite tough. I never really got to know her well in Indiana but I knew that she could smoke and drink with the best of the boys. Yet, she always looked out for me and did things that had a way of making me feel special. She was also a great help around the house. She cooked, cleaned, and even made a dress for me. She also encouraged me to paint my room and after I chose the color yellow she helped me paint it. She was very special to me. However, her three boys were another story. They were trouble with a capital T. Daddy referred to them as "Heathens."

The boys got in all kinds of trouble not only with Daddy but also with the law. And I got sucked in right along with them. Once they stole a monkey out of a cage. It lived in a cage outside of someone's house. They told me it was being abused and that's why they took it; Somehow two adults came and took it away from them and when I went to claim it from the adults they said they were going to call the cops on us for stealing. Another time the boys stole a bee-bee gun and this time I told them they had to return it! I wasn't about to let them continue on in a stealing rampage. But first, before they returned it to the owner, I thought it would be fun to try and shoot it. I had never shot a gun before so why not give it a try. As I stood at the edge of the creek, dressed in a red baseball hat, white painter's paints and a baseball jersey, I shot the gun at an old "abandoned" house and shed across the creek. (The boys told me it was abandoned.) I was a pretty good shot and therefore decided to shoot it a few more times. Suddenly a man ran out of the house with his own gun and we all scattered for safety. He never shot at us and the heathens and I laughed all the way home. They stopped on the way and dropped the gun in the owners yard. I felt as though I had done a good deed. However, as it had turned out; the man that ran out of his house had called the police and told them that a boy with white pants and a baseball jersey was shooting at his shed. (My long blond hair was tucked up under my hat when the shooting occurred.) That evening a cute young man on a dirt bike rode up wearing white pants and a baseball jersey. I didn't even realize that we were dressed similar until he said that he was arrested for stealing a bee-bee gun and identified by his clothes. When I heard him tell of what happened, my mouth dropped to the ground and he immediately realized it was me that he was mistaken for. After that day, Monty and I became friends.

The night before I was to leave for Florida for a short summer vacation I felt lonely. I sat outside under the stars starring up at Heaven. Even though I had friends and Daddy, something was missing in my life. I continued to get in trouble and make poor decisions. I felt guilty for betraying Daddy, God and for lying about the things I did. I sat outside with the warm breeze in my hair, the stars sparkling up above and a solid tree against my back and I spoke to God.

73
God Works All Things For The Good
August, 1979

I thought that when I moved to Texas I would start a new life; become a better person. By moving away I thought that *I* could change my old behaviors and habits. However, the temptations of alcohol and others attacked me soon after I moved to Texas. I relied on myself and I found out that it just wasn't enough. Before I thought that most of my troubles stemmed from the emotional or physical abuse. I blamed Mama for a lot of my troubles. I thought that the negative influence of friends brought me into temptation and trouble. But moving away to Texas taught me that it wasn't Mama or alcohol or friends that brought the guilt and bad things into my life.

That one night in Texas that I sat outside under the stars and spoke to God, I asked, "What am I doing? I know what is wrong, yet I continue to mess things up!" I knew he wanted more for me. Why did I always choose the wrong way? I cried. I prayed. I asked Jesus to please step into my life and take over. I asked Him for strength and to please help me start over, <u>one more time</u>. Soon after that prayer I went back to Florida to vacation with Mama and see my brothers.

While I was still vacationing in Florida, Daddy called me from Texas with news. He had been transferred again. This time to a place I knew nothing about. Before I could even fly back to Texas, he would be moving to Minnesota. He said that he was leaving our furniture with Bonnie and that he would pack all my personal items and move them for me. When I first heard the news about moving to Minnesota, I didn't like it at all. I even told Daddy that I would rather stay in Florida. I asked everyone if I could live with them, but they all knew I would be better off with Daddy. Mama was still living on the wild side and the boys didn't have a lifestyle fit to raise a teenage girl.

After I realized that I had no other option than to move to Minnesota, I decided to make the best of it. Though I doubted God wanted to up root me again and move me across the United States, in the back of my mind the thought occurred that this could be the answer to my prayer. Perhaps He knew that I couldn't start over in Cove, Texas. Of course, God knew what I could and could not handle, and I decided to trust that He had something better for me far away in what I thought was a frozen land where the sun never would shine.

Before leaving Florida, I made a vow that I wouldn't do anything more with guys until marriage. Late in August, I flew to Minnesota to establish my new life and I prayed that God would enable me to be the person that He created me to be.

Romans 8:28 (NIV)
And we know that in all things God works
for the good of those who love him,
who have been called according to His
purpose.

Epilogue

Minnesota wasn't as frozen as I thought it would be. And the sun did shine; it shone beautifully! Though I missed the warmth of the sunny beaches of Florida, I couldn't help but feel that God had brought me to where He wanted me to be. Just a few months after my move I saw snow cover the earth for the first time. It brought tears to my eyes to see how beautiful and clean everything could become. It reminded me of how God sent Jesus to die for our sins. Just as the snow fell and in a few short hours everything turned from dirty brown and ugly to beautifully white and crystal clean; the same was true with my Savior, Jesus. He came to earth and in the few hours that he hung on that cross every horrid sin of every believer turned from the tarnished brass hardness to clean clear beauty. We were forgiven and wiped clean of our dirt; our sins.

I know that it wasn't Minnesota that saved my life, nor was it my own determination. In fact, God changed my life the day I asked Him to come into my heart at the age of seven. Though I wasn't always obedient to Him or His Word.

Just a few years after I asked God into my heart, I basically departed from Him. He gave me the Holy Spirit to comfort me and He gave me His Word to guide me from temptation but truthfully, I didn't realize that God had given me either of those gifts. I relied on myself, and I failed. I gave in to sin: anger, bitterness and temptation and I turned away from God. During that time, my life was miserable. The Holy Spirit convicted me of my sin and I knew that I had done something wrong. Finally, while in Texas I cried out to God one more time. I asked forgiveness for my sins and I sought Jesus to be in control of my life. God heard my cries. He listened and he brought me back to Him.

> *2 Chronicles 7:14 (NIV)*
> *"If my people, who are called by my name, will humble themselves and pray and seek my face and turn from their wicked ways then will I hear from heaven and forgive their sin and heal their land."*

There were many good years in Minnesota. And then one day, I decided to break my vow to God regarding promiscuity. The circle of departing from God started all over again. That will have to be an entirely different book. But let me leave you with this. God has chosen His people. He choose me to be a Christian. At age seven I accepted His invitation. Then I left God to venture out on my own. I found out that I couldn't do it and returned to Him early in my teens. Then in college I departed again. It was a vicious circle that I followed at least a half a dozen times. Now I can tell you that I have returned to God again! In Malachi 3:7 God tells us, *"Return to me, and I will return to you."* Praise the Lord, He never put a limit to the number of times we can return to Him.

Many years passed as I struggled with something deep inside that continued to haunt me. What was it that kept me from being truly one with the Lord? It was unforgiveness. It was the bitterness that I carried around regarding Mama and many others. (Daddy passed away in 1988. He died from pancreatitis which is caused by alcoholism.) Then I remembered how many times God had forgiven me. Not just once, or twice but practically seventy times seven. Bible verses came to me of how we are to forgive our trasspassers. Yet, I thought I had the right to be angry. I had the right not to honor my parents because they didn't bring me up in a good Christian home. They didn't do what I thought they should have done. I was a victim, right? Wrong. I was and am a child of God.

Shortly before my 27th birthday I began to have dreams that I would never live to see the age of 27. The dreams reoccurred night after night and that's when I realized that if I was going to meet my maker, I wanted to have things cleared up here on earth first. Doesn't Romans tell us not to let the sun go down on our anger? Well there had been too many sunsets for my angry heart. So I sought to rebuild my relationship with Mama. I found out that she doesn't remember hardly any of the past and what she does remember she chooses not to talk about. That is very okay with me. I love Mama for who she is, and I seek to find the good in her today and the good she showed me as a child. The memories are just the past. I need not stay and dwell on them, only think of her as my sister in Christ and I know how wonderful she truly is.

Today, I seek God daily, I submit myself every morning to Him. I read His Word to guide me and rely on the Holy Spirit to comfort me. I pray that I never depart from Him again! I continue to read many Christian books to help me stay on track. Charles Sheldon wrote a book entitled, *IN HIS STEPS* and this book helped me a great deal. I would also recommend Neal Anderson's *THE BONDAGE BREAKER*. Now I really try to serve the Lord in everything I do. He helps me to be the best servant, wife and mother that He alone can guide me to be.

I hope that this book has touched you in some way. It was written to glorify God and to exemplify His working hand in all of our lives. You may look into your own past and see similarities to the problems associated with abuse, and rebellion. With confidence, I can assure

you that God wants more for you. My faith and assurance lies in this promise;
I Corinthians 10:13 (NIV)
No temptation has seized you except what is common to man. And God is faithful; he will not let you be tempted beyond what you can bear. But when you are tempted, he will also provide a way out so that you can stand up under it.

Please, as you close this book, remember to reach to someone that may be hurting and forgive those who may have hurt you. Begin the healing process today by: humbling yourself, seek God's face, and asking forgiveness for sins. Remember that anger and bitterness can be strongholds in your life and ask God to forgive you for not forgiving others. Go back to God and He will bring you to the light beyond the darkness!

SALVATION PRAYER

Lord, I come to you as a sinner. I have sinned and I seek your forgiveness. I know that Jesus Christ, your son came into this world and died for all my sins and suffering. And now I desire a fresh start- I don't want to sin any longer. I want to be a better person, but I can't do it on my own. I need you Lord. I pray now for Jesus to enter into my heart. God, I ask that you would forgive me of my sins and I pray that you would send the Holy Spirit to guide me in all ways.

Signature_____

date_____

If you have just said this prayer- please write to me so that I can pray for you and know that I have a new brother or sister in Christ!

T.C. Morton
Solid Rock Publishing
P.O. Box 913
Stillwater, MN 55082

To Mama:
> *Mama, I love you.*
> *Not for the hugs that I needed and you*
> *couldn't give.*
> *Not for the nights that I prayed that I*
> *wouldn't live.*
>
> *Mama, I love you.*
> *Not for the addiction over which you*
> *had no control.*
> *Not for your temper that often*
> *took its toll.*
>
> *Mama, I love you.*
> *In spite of the memories*
> *that shadow my mind,*
> *forgiveness is all*
> *that my heart can find.*
>
> *So, Mama, I love you.*
> *Not for yesterday*
> *So full of strife,*
> *I love you for showing me Jesus;*
> *the Way, the Truth and the Life.*